W0247056

PENGUIN BOOKS
KIDNAPPED

Arita Sarkar is a journalist based out of Mumbai. Since 2011, she has been a reporter at *The Hindu*, *Mumbai Mirror*, the *Indian Express* and *Mid-Day*. Her interest in cases concerning the Juvenile Justice Act, the Protection of Children from Sexual Offences (POCSO) Act and child rehabilitation led her to research and write a book about the widespread kidnapping of children in India.

After completing her schooling from the American International School/Dhaka, she graduated from Delhi University with a degree in English literature and later attended the Asian College of Journalism in Chennai. Apart from being a writer, she is an ardent lover of music and food and loves to dabble in a bit of both.

ARITA SARKAR

KIDNAPPED

TRUE STORIES OF
ABDUCTION, RANSOM AND REVENGE

**BLUE
SALT**

PENGUIN BOOKS

An imprint of Penguin Random House

PENGUIN BOOKS

USA | Canada | UK | Ireland | Australia
New Zealand | India | South Africa | China | Singapore

Penguin Books is part of the Penguin Random House group of companies
whose addresses can be found at global.penguinrandomhouse.com

Published by Penguin Random House India Pvt. Ltd
4th Floor, Capital Tower 1, MG Road,
Gurugram 122 002, Haryana, India

First published in Penguin Books by Penguin Random House India and
Blue Salt Media 2019

Copyright © Arita Sarkar 2019

10 9 8 7 6 5 4 3 2

The views and opinions expressed in this book are the author's own and the facts
are as reported by her which have been verified to the extent possible, and the
publishers are not in any way liable for the same.

ISBN 9780143442677

Typeset in Adobe Caslon Pro by Manipal Digital Systems, Manipal

Printed at Repro India Limited

www.penguin.co.in

*To Anandana Kapur, for being a solid sounding board,
to my family, for supporting the choices I have made in life,
and to all the children who never made it back home.*

Contents

Introduction   ix

1. Tarannum Fatema (Junera) Khan, Mumbai   1
2. Ritesh and Mukta, Coimbatore   29
3. Tanya Patel, Nadiad   51
4. Utkarsh Verma, New Delhi   71
5. Abhay Modani, Hyderabad   97
6. Franshela Vaz, Mumbai   119
7. Yash Lakhotia, Howrah   139
8. Adit Ranka, Mumbai   161
9. Om Kharat, Pune   187
10. Anant Gupta, Noida   211

Acknowledgements   231

Introduction

Back in 1953, when the National Crime Records Bureau (NCRB) published its first report, 5261 cases of kidnapping were reported that year. By 1994, the NCRB included a separate chapter on crimes against children. Apart from cases of kidnapping, the chapter provided state-wise data on the broader categories of crimes such as infanticide, rape and murder. That year, 864 cases had been filed wherein a child had been abducted.

In 2013, the Supreme Court passed a judgment that made it compulsory for the police to register all cases of missing children (as First Information Reports [FIRs]) and treat them as cases of kidnapping or trafficking. A significant increase was noted as the figure shot up from 28,167 in 2013 to 38,555 in the following year. With more awareness, more people reported crimes. But as far as kidnapping cases are concerned, the police say not much can be done to deter criminals. So, while the increase in numbers was a cause for concern, it didn't really change the way the police treat the cases. It was merely an indication that more people had come forward to report them. Individually, all cases where kidnapping of a child is involved are taken up on a priority basis.

It wasn't until 2014 that the NCRB decided to dedicate a chapter exclusively to kidnapping- and abduction-related statistics, which included data sorted by age group, sex and around fourteen kinds of motives. The number of child victims continued to grow substantially and as of 2016, the most current statistics available at the time of publishing, the figure stood at 54,328, with the highest number of cases reported in Uttar Pradesh.

Kidnapping is a serious offence, and according to the Indian Penal Code (IPC), it attracts a punishment of imprisonment that can extend up to seven years. Another section of the IPC specifically refers to kidnapping for ransom where a person is detained and the kidnapper threatens to kill or harm the victim. The punishment for this kind of offence could be a life or even a death sentence.

This book includes cases where multiple serious offences have been committed in a single case. For instance, in one of them, a child was kidnapped, raped and then murdered. In such extreme cases, the accused may be sentenced to life or even death.[1]

The annual reports are an essential source of information for the government since the data helps them understand the extent of the problem and accordingly maintain law and order

---

[1] After a sessions court pronounces its verdict, the accused has the option of appealing against the lower court's judgment in the high court and subsequently in the Supreme Court. In cases where an accused is acquitted or the quantum of punishment is less than expected, the state or even family members of the victim can then approach a higher court to appeal against the judgment.

in the country. Highlighting its importance, Meeran Chadha Borwankar, a retired IPS (Indian Police Service) officer and former director general of the NCRB, said that the Centre and state governments both rely on data collected by the NCRB from the State Crime Records Bureau (SCRB), which helps to understand crime patterns.

She added that many in the police force feel that increase and decrease in data on crimes does not reflect the true picture, since most cases in India go unreported. While the observation rings true in the case of petty crimes like thefts and chain snatching, Meeran finds the data on serious crimes like murders, kidnapping for ransom, fatal accidents and dacoities, among others, to be fairly accurate since nearly all the cases are reported. 'It may have a few deficiencies that we constantly strive to overcome but the NCRB statistics provide the basis for all crime-related discussions. The states depend on the data for crime analysis and developing strategies, while the Ministry of Home Affairs in New Delhi depends on the NCRB to deal with all-India crime patterns or analysis,'[2] she said.

As per the IPC, since there are different sections for the same offence, a logical classification of section-wise data can help the policymakers amend the existing laws for the prevention of specific crimes. In order to deploy police forces effectively, the state and central governments have to know the status of crime rates in every state. The information is useful to the government as well as the general public, especially citizen activists.

---

[2] From an email interview with Meeran Chadha Borwankar on 29 July 2018.

K.P. Asha Mukundan, a professor in the department of criminology and correctional administration at the Tata Institute of Social Sciences in Mumbai, said that the data is pivotal for research in order to understand the nuances of criminal activity in the country. 'Since the data is available, citizens don't have to file an RTI [Right to Information] application to get access to the crime rates in their city or state. The data is also required when someone has to file a PIL [public interest litigation] in court,'[3] she said.

Inaccuracies and manipulation of data

The data, however, is not an accurate picture of reality. In India, people are generally unwilling to get involved with the police, and as a result many cases go unreported. Akhilesh Kumar, former chief statistical officer at the NCRB, said, 'Based on the trend in developing countries, only 60 per cent of the crimes are being registered while the rest are unaccounted for. Due to the social stigma that exists in our society, people don't want to be involved in the lengthy process of registering a complaint.'[4]

As helpful as the NCRB's crime records are, there are several flaws the administration has not been able to address till date. In fact, at the beginning of every annual report, there is a disclaimer that says that the NCRB is not responsible for the authenticity of the data since it is only compiled and collated as provided by the states.

---

[3] From a telephonic interview with K.P. Asha Mukundan on 25 July 2017.

[4] From a telephonic interview with Akhilesh Kumar on 8 August 2017.

The data currently collected from police stations across the country only includes the number of the FIR that has been registered, which only takes cognizable crimes (serious offences like murder and rape) into consideration. Another former NCRB official, who didn't wish to be named, said that the NCRB doesn't count non-cognizable offences or petty crimes (for instance, public nuisance, simple hurt or mischief), which leaves out a significant number of cases.

The method of counting the 'principal offence' is possibly the most commonly debated flaw.

While counting the number of cases, only the principal offence or the charge that attracts the maximum penalty is taken into consideration. Journalists, activists and even the NCRB officials agree that this practice has led to undercounting of the number of cases. 'While there is no suppression of the number of cases in the data, misclassification might contribute to undercounting of the cases. For instance, if there is a case of kidnapping and murder, the case will only be counted once in the murder column,' said the NCRB official.

In their statement published in an article by *The Hindu*, however, the NCRB denied undercounting or underestimating crime figures and claimed that counting the principal offence 'is an internationally followed practice'. The official further claimed that the NCRB had no other method of counting to adopt other than the principal offence rule 'primarily due to the manual system of data collection in India'.[5]

Adding to the list of lacunae, the NCRB official referred to Section 153 (b) of the Code of Criminal Procedure of 1973 and

---

[5] https://www.thehindu.com/opinion/op-ed/ncrb-follows-international-practice-to-count-crime/article5135345.ece

pointed out that the court has the power to register cases directly and start trials. The NCRB, however, collects data only from police stations and does not include this source in their counting.

Barring counting errors, journalists have long argued the corruption of data, which can be attributed to political intervention especially around the elections. Jitendra Sharma, a senior journalist from Zee News who has covered crime in New Delhi for fourteen years, described the ways in which the data can be manipulated at police stations in the country's capital. 'For politicians, law and order is the most prominent subject of discussion, followed by corruption. The issues around law and order affect citizens on a day-to-day basis, which is why the state tends to downplay the data especially ahead of the elections,' he said.

For instance, Jitendra said that in most cases when the police come across an unidentified dead body, they don't investigate or count it as a case of murder. The police also try to downplay the number of cases related to snatching. 'They register an FIR for a small number of cases and the rest are registered either as a verbal complaint or as a non-cognizable offence,' he said.

Furthermore, the NCRB takes more than six months to publish the report of the previous year, as a result of which lawmakers don't have access to the latest figures. In 2017, for instance, the report was published in September (data for the previous year), and the 2018 report is yet to be released. A senior official from the NCRB said that while their target is usually July, the report gets delayed. 'If we have all the data, then we need only fifteen to twenty days to complete the analysis and publish the report. Most of the states send in their data by the end of January. But even if one state defaults, we can't publish the report,' said the official. He added that in the past few years, the eastern states, including West Bengal, have been the last ones to send their data.

Despite the long-standing flaws, there have been attempts to find solutions to improve or add other supporting data to understand the reality on the ground. During the time Meeran was heading the NCRB, she felt that the feedback of the user's input was important. 'We have long been recommending a nationwide Crime Impact Study/Analysis, where a professional agency gets in touch with citizens through proper sampling method and finds out actual crime vis-à-vis reported crime,' she said. She also suggested that involving more academicians and field-level NGOs, especially for cases of human trafficking, can help improve data collection.

The NCRB officials said that the general public has a role to play in improving the authenticity of data, especially when it comes to statistics related to the kidnapping of children. 'After the Supreme Court ruling, all police stations have to mandatorily register cases of missing children as kidnapping cases. But in many of the cases, the children return home after a few hours or days. The parents, however, don't update the police about it and the case is counted,' said a senior NCRB official, requesting anonymity. He added that the police count the cases depending on the status as on 31 December.

Noted trends

When considering the data on kidnapping of children, however, a relatively small number of cases have ransom or revenge as the motive behind the crime. In 2016, for instance, of the total number of cases, 168 children were kidnapped for ransom while 250 were for revenge.

The NCRB officials attribute the comparatively small number of cases to parents' reluctance to report the disappearance of their children out of fear that the kidnappers would harm their child if they approach the police.

The gender-wise data of kidnapping cases for ransom and revenge as motives over the past three years also indicates that the number of cases involving boys has always exceeded those involving girls. For example, in 2016, 137 boys and thirty-one girls were kidnapped for ransom, and 177 boys and seventy-three girls were kidnapped for revenge. Similarly, in 2015, 112 boys and thirty-five girls were kidnapped for ransom while 107 boys and forty-eight girls were kidnapped for revenge.

Even though the NCRB doesn't provide a reason for the trend, Meeran feels that this has always been the pattern since kidnappers are usually men and keeping an abducted boy is always easier. 'Having a girl child around till ransom is settled raises suspicion of neighbours and people around. Girls are kidnapped in cases of human trafficking or when they are being forced into prostitution,' she said.

Unlike other heinous crimes, kidnapping cases are tricky since even after the crime has been committed, there is still a chance that the police will be able to save the child. But every case is unique. Senior police officials from various cities agree that the chances of the child returning home alive are much more if he or she has been kidnapped by a gang. Arup Patnaik, former police commissioner of Mumbai, said that when the kidnapper is a novice, they tend to panic when things don't go as per their plan.[6]

---

[6] From an interview with Arup Patnaik at Bandra Kurla Complex, Mumbai, on 10 August 2017.

Looking back at the cases he has handled in the past, Arup feels that the chances of finding a kidnapped child alive also depend on the child's age. 'A child who is two years old or younger will not remember much. But if the child is more than three years old, then the kidnappers know that the child will go back home and reveal their identity to the parents and the police. In such cases, the tendency is to kill the child first and then try to get the ransom amount,' he said.

When dealing with ransom cases, the police will usually allow the sum to be paid since their primary aim is to ensure that the child comes back home alive. Ashok Chand, former additional commissioner of police (crime), New Delhi, said that in cases where the police are unaware of the location of the victim, they don't interfere if the ransom is being paid by the family. 'We allow the deal to go through and once the child is back home, we go after the kidnappers,' he said.

Over the years, the use of technology has become an integral part of both the kidnapper's plan and the police's method of investigation. While kidnappers use voice-changing mobile applications to conceal their identity and SIM cards purchased against fake identity cards, the police rely heavily on the tracking of the phone's IMEI (International Mobile Equipment Identity) number and the CCTV footage of cameras in the neighbourhood.

Back in the day, as former Mumbai Police Commissioner Arup recalled, landline phones were the only mode of communication for the kidnappers. Referring to the case of Vatsal Shah, the eight-year-old boy who was kidnapped from his house at Juhu and murdered by two Dubai-based NRI brothers in July 1992, Arup pointed out that ransom calls were then made from a public phone booth. 'Landline phones have now been replaced by mobile phones. Forensic evidence can now be collected from details of the mobile handset and SIM cards. But technology has helped both the police as well as the kidnappers, and the smart ones will try to be a step ahead by doing things like changing SIM cards,'[7] he said.

The way forward

There are ways in which parents can keep a closer eye on their children. Meeran feels that by treating the staff at their workplace and at home in a good manner, parents can help reduce the chances of attracting unwanted attention which can leave their child in a vulnerable position. Arup recommends the use of technology to help parents keep track of their children. 'In some schools in New Delhi, students have been given RFID [Radio-Frequency Identification] tags which allow their parents to know the exact location of their child at all times for their safety,' he said.

Unlike cases of child trafficking, kidnapping cases are unpredictable, due to which the NCRB data cannot directly help the police curb the numbers, except perhaps to understand broad trends. But there are ways in which the legal system and the police can discourage the very idea of kidnapping innocent children or anyone else for that matter.

Chand pointed out that there is room for improvement in police investigation as well, which would ensure a stronger case to be presented in court.

---

[7] https://timesofindia.indiatimes.com/india/NRIs-get-lifer-for-murder-of-8-year-old/articleshow/1933450.cms

Meeran shares a similar view. She feels confident that speedy trials and proper documentation can help reduce the number of kidnapping cases in the country, especially when it comes to organized criminal gangs. 'The NCRB data shows that our conviction of such cases is less than 50 per cent. In most cases I feel families do not support prosecution out of fear, but we do need improvement in the conviction of such criminals,' she said. A collaborative attempt of state agencies can indicate that they take a firm stand, that they are intolerant to individuals who harm innocent children for ulterior motives.

The research for this book began with a simple Google search and then progressed to detailed interviews and long hours perusing lengthy legal documents. Compared to the original list of cases that I had drawn up, only half of them became actual chapters. The process of selecting the cases focused on the outlier, the case that stood out. Despite being kidnapping cases, all the chapters in the book also involved either murder or rape.

A girl went missing for more than two weeks in one of the cases, while in another, not one but two children were kidnapped by the same person. One case remains unsolved till date, and in another, the kidnapping of a small girl was plotted allegedly by an entire family. Be it ransom or revenge, each case reveals the different motives driving the kidnappers and offers us a glimpse into the mindset of a kidnapper. Some of the cases listed in the book are currently under trial while in a few others, the trial is yet to begin. The sequence of events is based on information compiled from the police, the families of the victims and the accused, among others.

People who agreed to be interviewed for the book were generous enough to openly share all the relevant information with the common hope that in the end, the readers may benefit from their experiences of dealing with such cases. While I hope that no one has to go through such a terrible ordeal, I too share their hope that if and when another child is kidnapped, family members will feel encouraged to approach the police who will deal with the investigation in a responsible manner and ensure that the perpetrators don't go unpunished.

1

Tarannum Fatema (Junera) Khan, Mumbai

Around 8.45 p.m. on 5 December 2016, the maulana of the Kazipura Masjid in Nagpada turned on the mosque's loudspeaker. The *isha namaz* (prayer) would begin around 9 p.m., but the maulana wasn't preparing to sound the azan, the Muslim call to prayer, just yet. Instead, he picked up the microphone and announced to the neighbourhood that Tarannum Fatema Khan, a three-year-old girl from the area, had been missing for a few hours. Anyone with information about her should contact him at once, he added.

The unusual and unscheduled announcement wasn't the Maulana's own idea, rather the outcome of an inspired bit of thinking by a seventeen-year-old boy, Haneef Qazi.[1] On hearing that his neighbours' youngest daughter had vanished, he decided to go to the mosque and request the maulana to spread the word.

Tarannum's parents were, understandably, not coping well. Her mother, Shahida, then thirty, had realized only

---

[1] Name changed since he is a juvenile accused.

around 8 p.m. that day that she hadn't seen her youngest child for quite some time. When Shahida was busy with housework, she would usually leave Tarannum in the care of her siblings—fifteen-year-old Muskaan, eleven-year-old Faizan and seven-year-old Khushboo.

Shahida lived in a double-storeyed building in which all the residents lived on the first floor, with shops occupying the ground floor. There were fourteen houses on the first floor along with a courtyard that everyone used as a common space and where the children played.

The fourteen families that lived there knew each other well enough to leave their doors open throughout the day. Every one of them was fond of Tarannum, whom they lovingly called Junera. If she wasn't bounding around the house, she was usually playing in the courtyard with the neighbours' children.

But that evening, no one—neither her siblings nor her neighbours nor her neighbours' children—knew where Junera was. When it was dinner time, Shahida asked Khushboo to check if she was in the courtyard. She wasn't. Puzzled, Khushboo called out to her baby sister but to no avail.

She went back inside and told her mother that she couldn't find Junera. Shahida, fighting a nascent panic, went from door to door asking her neighbours if they had seen her daughter. By the time she had knocked on the last of the thirteen doors, she was trembling. Her three-year-old wasn't in the building.

Though she couldn't imagine that Junera could have left the building without her, Shahida telephoned her husband, Mumtaz, around 9 p.m. to check if she had somehow made her way to his shop, a ten-minute walk from their house.

Thirty-five-year-old Mumtaz, who deals in scrap material and plywood, sensed the panic in his wife's voice at once. '*Junnu aayi kya dukan pe?* (Has Junnu come to the shop?)' she asked, praying he would say yes.

Mumtaz said he had last seen her playing in the corridor when he left for the shop at 1.30 p.m. Shahida broke down and told her husband that their youngest daughter had disappeared. Mumtaz rushed back home at once with some of his workers. On the way, one of them—Shiraz Hashmi—told him he had seen Junera at home when he had gone there a little before 8 p.m. to pick up a prescription for Mumtaz's medicines.

Mumtaz recalls, 'Junera had asked Shiraz to take her to the shop so she could meet me. He told her he had to buy some things first and would pick her up on his way back to the shop. But when he went back to the house with the medicines, Junera wasn't around. A few minutes later, my wife realized that she was missing.'[2]

Once home, Mumtaz, Shahida and the workers began to scour other buildings in the neighbourhood for any sign of the missing girl. News of her disappearance spread quickly among the neighbours and a few joined in the search. The enterprising Haneef thought of informing the local maulana and news of Junera's disappearance quickly spread to the rest of the locality. But all of this proved futile and about an hour later Mumtaz decided it was time to inform the police.

From the moment the mosque in Kazipura sounded the alarm, Mumtaz mustered up every ounce of strength he had

---

[2] From an interview with Mumtaz Khan in Mumbai on 10 March 2018.

to believe that he would find his daughter, using any means possible. He went to J.J. Marg police station around 10.30 p.m. to report that his three-year-old daughter had vanished.

As the police began to put together a team to find the missing girl, Mumtaz decided to expand his own search. He and his friends went to every bus stop in Nagpada and visited several train stations nearby, including Byculla and Chhatrapati Shivaji Maharaj Terminus (CSMT). Others scoured the hutments along Reay Road, all to no avail.

The frantic search continued through the night, but neither the police nor Mumtaz and his friends found any clue. The next morning the police registered a case of kidnapping.

One of the first things that Inspector Hemant Bavdhankar, one of the two investigating officers, looked for was CCTV camera footage from around the building. They found that a shop on the ground floor had a CCTV camera pointed in the direction of the entrance.

But the shop owner told the police that the camera stopped recording when he shut his shop at 9 p.m. every day. Nonetheless, they scanned hours of footage. In an interview for this book, Inspector Hemant said, 'From the footage we learnt that the girl had entered the building with her mother around 5.30 p.m. We also concluded that she couldn't have left the building before 9 p.m.'[3]

Next, the police turned their attention to the narrow lanes between the buildings. With the help of municipal officials, they opened up around thirty drains between Kazipura and Do Tanki. In one of these, near the Khans' building, they

---

[3] From an interview with Hemant Bavdhankar in Mumbai on 13 March 2018.

found their first clue—Junera's distinctive yellow slippers. But this was as far as they got.

The police asked Mumtaz if he could think of anyone—a rival or enemy—who could have a motive to kidnap his daughter. Mumtaz had no answer to this. His family had been living there since 2010, and he was on good terms with all his neighbours, relatives and acquaintances. 'I didn't know anybody who hated me enough to kidnap my daughter. When we found her slippers, I had faith that in time we would find her too,' he told me.

While searching in the neighbourhood, the police examined other possibilities too, including child trafficking. Dhiraj Bhalerao, a sub-inspector and the other investigating officer in the case, said they also looked into the local vendors as well as beggars who lived in the area. But they had no luck.

After Junera's slippers were found, the police even brought sniffer dogs to the building, but they too were unable to find any trace of the missing girl.

With no other clues in sight, the police began questioning the Khans' neighbours.

They collected the phone numbers and photographs of all the youngsters, despite objections from their families. Among them was seventeen-year-old Haneef. Dhiraj recalled asking him if he had seen Junera that day, to which Haneef replied that he had last seen her in the afternoon playing in the courtyard.

Ten days went by and no one had heard or seen the three-year-old. It wasn't until 16 December that the police came across a potential lead to pursue. Haneef telephoned Manoj Kumar Sharma, deputy commissioner of police (DCP) (zone 1) on 16 December and told him he had seen three strangers—two men and a woman—right outside his building on the day

Junera was taken. Suspicious, he had eavesdropped on them and realized that they were talking about a child.

Desperate for leads, the DCP instructed the local police to get descriptions of the three from Haneef and put together a search team.

Dhiraj and other police officials spent the night checking houses in Dongri, Nagpada and other areas along Mohammed Ali Road under the J.J. flyover and eventually detained three people from Nagpada—a married couple and their friend—for questioning. All three of them claimed to know nothing about the girl's disappearance.

Their suspicions were piqued when one of the neighbours of the arrested people they questioned said she had seen a young girl visit the married couple's home in Nagpada some time ago. Dhiraj said, 'Based on this information, we rounded up all the children in the neighbourhood and gave them chocolates. We showed them pictures of a few children, including the missing girl, and asked them if they recognized any of them.'[4] But they didn't. The police had no choice but to release the three suspects.

* * *

Life had come to a standstill for the Khans. Shahida stayed at home with the three children, who refused to go to school, while Mumtaz continued to search for his missing daughter, chasing every rumour like it was a solid lead. Over the next few days, he and his relatives searched for her as far away as Goregaon,

---

[4] From an interview with Dhiraj Bhalerao in Mumbai on 13 March 2018.

Panvel, Kalyan and Mankhurd. 'A religious leader we consulted said that we would find her in Pune so we even went there to look for her,' he said. But he found no trace of his daughter there.

After consulting with the police, Mumtaz and his relatives printed out posters with Junera's photograph and a contact number. They put up around 500 of these near mosques, dargahs, temples and other buildings at various locations, including Mumbai Central, Bandra and Mahim.

At 2.10 p.m. on 19 December, a fortnight after Junera had gone missing, just when Mumtaz was slowly coming to terms with reality, his phone rang. On the line was a man who claimed to have kidnapped his daughter. In a call that lasted a few seconds, he told Mumtaz to arrange for Rs 1 crore if he wanted to see his daughter again. Before Mumtaz could so much as utter a word, the kidnapper hung up.

Dazed, Mumtaz rushed to J.J. Marg police station and met Sub-Inspector Dhiraj. After listening to what had happened, Dhiraj asked him to buy a mobile phone that could record calls. Mumtaz promptly did so. He also began to ask his relatives and friends to loan him money for the ransom.

Arranging for Rs 1 crore was out of the question but Mumtaz decided to put together whatever he could. But these were the early days of demonetization, which Prime Minister Narendra Modi had announced on 8 November 2016, and cash withdrawals were limited to Rs 24,000 a week. Putting together Rs 1 crore in cash, which would have been nearly impossible in normal times, was now truly out of the question.

The kidnapper telephoned Mumtaz again around 2.30 p.m. the next day and told him he had two days to arrange for the ransom. He warned Mumtaz to not involve the police. Hoping to strike a bargain, Mumtaz tried to reason with the kidnapper. But before he could begin to negotiate, the kidnapper disconnected the line. The call lasted just fifteen seconds.

The next day, 21 December, was Junera's fourth birthday. Under normal circumstances, she would be at home waiting to cut her cake and open her presents. Mumtaz tried his best to remain strong and spent the morning at home with his family, praying that she was safe and would be found soon.

At 3.30 p.m., Mumtaz received the third call from the kidnapper. 'Have the money ready by 2 p.m. on 23 December,' he said. Mumtaz begged him to reduce the ransom, saying it would be impossible to put together that much money in a couple of days. But the kidnapper refused to negotiate. He repeated his demand and hung up.

Distraught, Mumtaz spoke to the police, who said it was vital that he verify that his daughter was indeed with them and alive as it had been seventeen days since she had disappeared.

Mumtaz waited for the next call, ready to negotiate and to demand that the kidnapper put his daughter on the phone. As expected, he called again at 3.30 p.m. on 22 December.

Kidnapper: Have Rs 1 crore ready by 2 p.m. tomorrow. I will call again.

Mumtaz: Please hear me out. I don't have that kind of money. Please reduce the amount a little. I can't arrange for that much money.

Kidnapper: How much do you have?

Mumtaz: I only have a rented house and a small shop.

Kidnapper: Can you give Rs 80 lakh?

Mumtaz: Please try to understand. I don't have that much money.

Kidnapper: All right then. I'll chop off your daughter's hand
              and send it to you. Then you can sit and decide.
Mumtaz: Please, please don't do that. Please let me speak
              to my daughter.
Kidnapper: Have the money ready by 2 p.m. tomorrow.
Mumtaz: Please listen to me . . . please . . .[5]
[Kidnapper hangs up]

Mumtaz tapped every source and called up every person he
could think of but when the kidnapper called again, around
noon the next day, he was well short of the Rs 80 lakh ransom.

   Mumtaz begged him to reduce the amount further, saying
it was impossible to get that much money when the entire
country was in the midst of a cash crunch. This seemed to do
the trick. The kidnapper relented and agreed to settle for Rs
50 lakh. The police took this as a sign that he—or they—were
getting desperate.

   Over the next few hours, the kidnapper, now showing
urgency, called Mumtaz several times and asked how much
money he had managed to raise. Mumtaz said he had Rs 28
lakh. To his relief, the man told him to bring the money to
CSMT. 'They told me to take a bus to CSMT and get on a
train to Titwala, saying they would be waiting for me there,'
said Mumtaz. He said his afternoon prayers and left home
with the bag of money at 1.30 p.m.

   A team of plain-clothes policemen, comprising twenty
cops, went to CSMT and boarded the same train as Mumtaz.
Another group took up positions in and around Titwala
railway station. Mumtaz said, 'The scene was unreal—more

---

[5] Transcribed from the recordings of the telephonic conversations
    in Hindi.

like a movie than real life. One policeman was disguised as a shoe-polish man. Another pretended to be a snack-seller. Even I didn't know which of the people on the train were cops.' The third team, which included Inspector Hemant, travelled to Titwala station by road.

While dealing with kidnapping cases, Inspector Hemant mentioned to me that the police often have to rely on their gut feeling since no two cases are ever the same. There is always an element of unpredictability, which raises the stakes and makes it a bigger challenge for the police.

After studying the isolated spots along the train's route, Inspector Hemant suspected that the kidnappers would tell Mumtaz to drop the money in the tunnel just after Kalwa railway station. 'We told Mumtaz that if the kidnappers ordered him to do so, he should lie and tell them the train had crossed it.' When the kidnappers called, they asked exactly what Inspector Hemant had predicted and as advised, Mumtaz told them the train had already reached Mumbra.

While Mumtaz was on the train, the kidnappers called more than forty times and argued in many of the conversations. Mumtaz noticed that that voice of the person on the other end was different in some of the calls, which led him to conclude that more than one person was involved.

Though the kidnappers tried to convince Mumtaz to throw the bag out of the train while crossing the tunnel after Kalwa station, Mumtaz insisted that they let him speak to his daughter first. Despite his repeated requests, the kidnappers did not relent. They gave excuses and told him his daughter was being held in a car in an unconscious state.

When Mumtaz refused to throw the money without seeing his daughter or speaking to her, the kidnappers became agitated and started abusing him on the phone. They even threatened to kidnap another of his daughters. Mumtaz pleaded with them to take the money and give him his daughter in exchange. But they were adamant about getting the money first.

Kidnapper: We've been waiting here for three hours! If you throw the money out, you'll get your daughter at Kalwa. If not, you can forget about seeing her again. We are not c******s here.

Mumtaz: Do whatever you want to me but please let my daughter go.

Kidnapper: Listen to me. The girl was at Mumbra but now we have sent her to Kalwa in a car. We are here at the tunnel waiting for you. Throw the bag out and you'll get your daughter back.

Mumtaz: How can I believe that she is in the car? What guarantee do I have that you'll return her to me if I throw the money out?

Kidnapper: If you throw the money out, we'll give her back and you can take her back home. Look, it will take us less than a minute to kill her. Or we might sell her kidney and other organs first. But we don't want to do that. Just give us the money.

Mumtaz: She is an innocent girl . . . please . . .

Kidnapper: That is why we are sparing her.

This conversation continued over several phone calls. Two people took turns to speak to Mumtaz, urging him to throw the bag of money. One of them took an aggressive approach and tried to intimidate Mumtaz while the other tried to persuade him in a calm manner, telling him to do it for his daughter. In a last-ditch effort to pressurize Mumtaz, they claimed they were working for someone else, and that this person had told them not to let the girl go before they got the money. Between calls, Mumtaz shared the call recordings with the police on WhatsApp to keep them updated.

By the time he got off the train at Diva, a team of policemen were on their way to the tunnel near Kalwa station by road. Among them was Sub-Inspector Dhiraj.

They parked their vehicles on the Thane–Mumbra highway and approached the tunnel on foot. When they were just a few metres away, they saw a man walking out of the tunnel. He soon found himself surrounded by cops.

They took his phone and checked whether Mumtaz's number was in his call log. They soon realized he wasn't connected to the kidnapping and asked him if he had seen anyone else inside the tunnel. 'Yes,' the man replied—he had seen two boys in there who were talking to someone on the phone about money.

Dhiraj and the other policemen were unfamiliar with the area. He recalled how unsettled he had felt at the thought of going into the dark tunnel. 'The area was unknown to us. Though two of us had weapons, we didn't know how many people were in there. Our backup team hadn't arrived yet. We were going in blind,' said Dhiraj. They were also concerned that their sudden appearance—despite their civilian clothes—would cause the kidnappers to panic and harm Junera. But having come this far, they decided, it was a risk they would have to take.

The policemen walked into the tunnel with some trepidation. Before long, they saw what looked like two young men in the distance. But it was too late—the men had seen them too, and quickly hid in the darkness. Anticipating a gunfight, the policemen ducked for cover. By the time they stood back up, the two men were running in the direction of Gholai Nagar. The cops followed but the men were too quick. Around ten minutes into the chase, they came upon a young girl who told them she saw two men running out of the tunnel and getting into an autorickshaw.

The police began to scour the area and soon came across a rickshaw stand. They asked the drivers if any of them had recently picked up two male passengers. Eventually, they found a driver who said he had. He told them that the two men had asked him to take them to Kalwa station but changed their minds mid-journey and got down at Kharegaon toll naka instead.

Unfortunately, the Kharegaon toll naka doesn't have any CCTV cameras. The police had hit another dead end.

Based on the manner of their escape, and the accounts of people who had seen them, the police concluded that the kidnappers hadn't brought Junera along with them. On hearing the news, Mumtaz was more concerned than ever about his daughter's safety. 'I didn't know what to think any more. It felt like an unending nightmare,' he said.

Dhiraj recalled the concern he had of Mumtaz blaming him if his daughter was harmed or killed as he had told him not to part with the money unless the kidnappers gave him proof that she was alive and unharmed. Adding to his stress was pressure from the Mumbai police commissioner, Dattatray Padsalgikar, and the joint commissioner of police, Deven Bharti, who were displeased on hearing that the kidnappers had managed to flee.

With no other leads to chase, Dhiraj realized that after being so close to catching the suspects, they were back to square one. Determined not to give up, he returned to the police station at 11 p.m. that night and, with Constable Deepak Patil, spent the next eight hours analysing the call records of the kidnappers' phone. Their effort paid off when they found one of the numbers was that of Sabir Abdullah Dukka, the owner of Nice Mobile Corner at Shahin Bazaar near Bandra railway station.

Dhiraj said, 'Sabir told us that two boys, who seemed to be sixteen or seventeen years old, had bought a Rs 85 recharge voucher from him on 19 December. We showed him pictures of people who lived in Junera's building and he recognized one of them.'

The boy whose photo Sabir pointed to was none other than Haneef, who had seemed so eager—perhaps too eager, in retrospect—to help find the missing girl. Dhiraj realized that the idea to have news of Junera's disappearance spread through the mosque's public address system and the tip-off about the suspicious trio outside the Khans' building had all been a ploy to avert suspicion and mislead the police.

It was clear to Dhiraj that this was no ordinary seventeen-year-old. However, he had slipped up. After buying the talktime voucher, Haneef had called Sabir's number to check if he was able to make calls. A single error had put the police on his trail.

Simultaneously, the police started looking through the call data records of around seventy-five people who lived in or around the Khans' building. After going through the details of 6540 phone calls that night, Dhiraj came across calls between Haneef and another likely suspect—Saif Rehman,[6] a sixteen-

---

[6]   Name changed since he is a juvenile accused.

year-old boy who lived nearby. The police then checked the location of their phones around the time Mumtaz was on his way to drop off the ransom. Sure enough, their cell tower locations showed they were at Kalwa.

Though the police had now found enough evidence to strongly suspect that Haneef and Saif had kidnapped Junera, they kept this information to themselves and came up with a plan.

On 24 December, they took several teenage boys and men from the neighbourhood to the police station in batches. Dhiraj said, 'All we told them was that senior police officials had asked us to question the Khans' neighbours. Our aim was to find Junera; catching the culprits was secondary.'

When the police went to Haneef's house in the evening, he was nowhere to be found—only his grandmother and twelve-year-old sister were at home. When Dhiraj asked where he was, his sister said he had gone with their parents and aunt to a *peer baba* in Andheri. The cops suspected that the boy's parents knew what he had done, but said nothing.

Dhiraj came up with another plan—to make Haneef's parents return home with him without arousing their suspicion. For that, they would have to fake an emergency. He managed to convince the girl to tell her father that her grandmother had fallen ill.

But when she spoke to her father on the phone, he seemed suspicious. 'To check if she was telling the truth, he told her that she would lose her eyesight if she lied to him. After hanging up the phone, the girl began to cry. We explained to her that nothing of that sort would happen and she agreed to try again,' said Dhiraj.

However, the girl was unable to convince her father to return home. He telephoned a relative and their family doctor and told them to check if his mother was indeed ill. When they arrived, the police took them into confidence and persuaded them to confirm what the girl had said. It was only after getting confirmation from the doctor that Haneef's parents decided to return.

When they walked into the building, the police were ready. They detained Haneef and took him to the police station for questioning.

* * *

At first, Haneef denied knowing anything about Junera's kidnapping. Then, the police claimed, he began making up various contradictory stories. Dhiraj said, 'Initially, he put the blame on another resident of the building, who he said had six daughters and believed in magic. But then he changed his story. He said that six other people were involved in the girl's kidnapping and if he told the police the truth, they would kill him.'

Soon, the boy began to get entangled in his own lies. Four hours into his questioning, he confessed that he had kidnapped Junera. When asked where she was, Haneef said he had killed her.

'Had we not arrested him, he could have become a hardened career criminal. He had the brains for it and it's a shame. If he used his talents for something constructive, he would have been successful in life,' said Dhiraj.

After Haneef, it was Saif's turn to be questioned. Unlike in Haneef's case, the police's findings indicated that Saif had nothing to do with Junera's murder, but they suspected he had helped Haneef plan her kidnapping. The police already knew that Saif was in Kalwa on 23 December, when Mumtaz was on his way there with the ransom.

When they asked Saif where he had been in the past few days, he told them that his exams were coming up and that he had been busy studying at home. But when asked whether he had travelled to Thane recently, he first denied it and then made up a story. 'He said he had a brother who lived there and had asked him to come over. We asked him to show us the phone calls or messages between him and his brother. But he wasn't able to show us anything,' said Dhiraj.

The boy eventually told the police that Haneef, after killing Junera, had telephoned him and managed to convince him to make some of the ransom calls to Mumtaz.

As other details surfaced, the police were able to piece it all together.

On 5 December, the police said, Haneef was alone at home when he spotted Junera playing by herself outside her house. He lured the girl into his flat by promising her chocolates. Once inside, he used chloroform, which he had apparently stolen from his college, to render her unconscious. 'When her sister and mother came to look for her, Haneef panicked and strangled her with the wire of his mobile charger,' said Hemant.

After killing Junera, Haneef allegedly stuffed her body in a blue bag, around 1.5 x 1.5 feet, and hid it behind two water tanks on the terrace of an adjoining building just 5 feet away from his own window. According to the police, he threw the bag on to the adjoining terrace before climbing over to hide it behind the tanks.

The police, during their search of the neighbourhood shortly after Junera's disappearance, didn't check the terraces of the adjoining buildings but took the sniffer dogs only around the buildings. The body remained undetected for twenty days after the murder.

By the time Haneef led them to her body on 24 December, it had severely decomposed. As a result, the post-mortem, conducted at Sir J.J. Hospital, failed to ascertain the cause of death. Her viscera were sent to Delhi's Forensic Science Laboratory, which is yet to release its final report.

The police were now left with the excruciating task of telling Junera's parents that their little girl would not come back home. DCP Manoj knew it wasn't the kind of news that could be broken over the phone. Around midnight on 24 December, he telephoned Mumtaz and told him to come to the police station with Shahida.

When they arrived, DCP Manoj called Mumtaz to a room while his wife, younger brother and sister waited outside. After offering him a glass of water, the DCP asked if he had received any other calls from the kidnappers. Mumtaz said he hadn't.

He then broke the news to him. 'He told me that my daughter had been kidnapped and then murdered by one of my neighbours' sons. I couldn't understand anything else he said after that,' Mumtaz recalls. The police asked Mumtaz to accompany them to J.J. Hospital to identify the body that had been found.

Steeling himself, Mumtaz decided that it was better if he went to the hospital alone. 'I figured that it would be better if I told my wife about what had happened back home. So I didn't tell her or my sister anything at the police station and asked them to go back home,' he said. After he returned from the hospital, Mumtaz broke the news to his wife.

Haneef and Saif were formally taken into custody early on 25 December and later sent to the children's observation home at Umerkhadi.

Over the next few days, the police formed a clearer picture of why, and how, Junera was kidnapped and murdered. Haneef confessed that he had abducted her for money, and killed her just a few hours later when Shahida began going from door to door looking for her. He told the police that killing her wasn't part of his original plan and that he did so because he had panicked.

The police said Haneef had begun planning the kidnapping a couple of months before. 'He said he often saw Mumtaz's relatives visit him in expensive cars and assumed that Mumtaz too was a wealthy man. Junera, who often played right outside his house, was an easy target,' said Hemant. He recollected the case as one of the goriest he had seen in his career.

Both Haneef and Saif were science students at a junior college in south Mumbai and, according to the police, wanted to set up a business of their own.

Haneef's kidnapping plan started with the purchase of a Nokia 1100 mobile phone from Chor Bazaar on 16 November. He then allegedly shared his scheme with his friend Saif. Saif, however, came into the picture only after Junera's death, at the time when the ransom calls were being made.

A newspaper mentioned that the police claimed Haneef was fond of sports cars and had wanted to purchase a Mercedes Benz. The report further added that both Haneef and Saif had planned to divide the money and use it to buy a sport bike.[7]

---

[7] https://www.mid-day.com/articles/mumbai-crime-mumbai-news-mumbai-murder-toddler-killed-rs-1-crore-ransom/17862188

Saif also told the police that they had tried to rope in another friend. 'Saif and Haneef had told one of their friends to track Mumtaz on the train. He, however, didn't go and instead told another friend to do it. This person was shown a picture of Mumtaz and told that he was carrying some important documents that belonged to Haneef. Both boys are now witnesses in the case,' said Dhiraj.

* * *

One fact left the police baffled. For almost three weeks, nobody in either of the buildings had noticed the smell emanating from Junera's decomposed body. Mumtaz said this was because the first-floor flat of the adjoining building had been vacant for a year.

But Haneef's father told the police that he had noticed the foul odour and told his son about it. From then on, the police said, Haneef would go to the spot where he had hidden the body and sprinkle attar on it every day.

The police investigation also revealed that Haneef had bought four SIM cards from a shop in Ghatkopar on 16 December, and two of them had a fake identity proof on record. The vendor who sold the SIM cards to them later identified them and is also one of the witnesses in the case.

* * *

On 22 August 2017, the Juvenile Justice Board ordered that Haneef be tried as an adult and Saif as a juvenile. This was after the amended Juvenile Justice (Care and Protection) Act, 2015, wherein children aged between sixteen and eighteen were to be tried as adults in certain cases, came into effect in January 2016.[8]

Special public prosecutor Shishir Hirey said this was one of the first cases in Mumbai in which a juvenile was facing trial as an adult.[9]

---

[8] The Juvenile Justice (Care and Protection) Act, 2015, was drafted subsequent to the debate that followed two gang rape cases involving minors—one committed in Delhi in December 2012, which came to be known as the Nirbhaya case, and the other, Mumbai's Shakti Mills case, in August 2013.

As per the new act, Section 15 states that given the 'heinous' nature of some crimes committed by juveniles, perpetrators aged between sixteen and eighteen should be tried as adults.

The new act calls for a preliminary assessment of the alleged offender by the Juvenile Justice Board, which seeks the help of psychologists or psychosocial workers to 'assess the capacity of a juvenile to commit and understand the consequences of the alleged offence'.

Based on the assessment, the board will determine if the child should be tried as an adult. In the event that this is the finding, the case will be transferred to a children's court which will decide if there is a need for a trial or further inquiry.

The act states that if found guilty, the children's court cannot sentence the child to death or life imprisonment. If tried before the board for serious crimes, the child can be sentenced to a maximum of three years in a reformative home as was the norm in the previous version of the act for all cases. See https://indianexpress.com/article/india/kidnap-and-murder-of-girl-in-nagpada-17-year-old-will-be-tried-in-childrens-court-says-juvenile-justice-board-4810771/; https://mumbaimirror.indiatimes.com/mumbai/crime/trying-a-child-as-an-adult-wont-reform-the-offender/articleshow/48194766.cms; and the text of the Juvenile Justice Act, 2015.

[9] From an interview with Shishir Hirey in Mumbai on 19 March 2018.

Hirey said he had asked the court to allow both Haneef and Saif to be tried as adults but P.R. Shinde, the principal magistrate of the City Juvenile Justice Board, ruled that Saif should not be tried as an adult. In his order, he stated that this was because only Haneef was suspected of kidnapping and killing Junera while Saif's role was allegedly limited to helping Haneef with the ransom calls.

The magistrate also took into consideration a social investigation report, filed by probation officers, which noted that neither boys had a prior criminal record. The report also included an assessment of the boys' physical and mental capacities, and stated that both were capable of understanding the consequences of their actions.

Haneef's lawyer, Nitin Sejpal, challenged the magistrate's ruling in the Bombay High Court, saying it would be too harsh on his client to try him as an adult.[10] He said, 'Just because the Juvenile Justice Act was amended, it doesn't necessarily mean that all juveniles must be tried as adults. If convicted, Haneef will come in contact with hardened criminals, which will increase the chances of him becoming one of them.'

Meanwhile, Rizwan Merchant, who represented the prosecution at the Bombay High Court, objected to the Juvenile Justice Board's decision to try Saif as a juvenile. Saif was granted bail on 25 August 2017, while Haneef remains in custody.

Shishir defended the prosecution stand on trying both boys as adults by arguing that their individual roles wouldn't be viewed in isolation. 'The court always considers a person's

---

[10] From an interview with Nitin Sejpal in Mumbai on 21 March 2018.

individual role in a crime and it won't convict them at the same level. Having two separate trials for the same case is not a good idea,' he said.

He also said that it would be unfair to ask the witnesses to appear in two separate trials. 'Any changes, omissions or contradictions in their statements would harm the prosecution's case. Besides, why should the complainant suffer twice? Mumtaz has already lost his daughter. He should not be made to suffer more,' Shishir added.

Though there were no eyewitnesses to Junera's kidnapping or murder, and the evidence gathered by the police was largely circumstantial, Shishir said the prosecution had a strong case. The evidence included call records and statements of witnesses. Among the witnesses was an eleven-year-old girl who lived in the same building as the Khans. A fortnight after Junera went missing, the police claimed that she told them that she had seen Junera go to Haneef's house on 5 December. But the public prosecutor himself called this into question.

Shishir added, however, that voice samples collected from Haneef and Saif matched the voices in Mumtaz's recordings of the ransom calls. The kidnappers had made nearly sixty phone calls over five days using multiple phone numbers.

He added that an empty bottle had been found in the bag which contained Junera's body and that the police suspected it had contained chloroform.

Nitin, however, argued that Haneef had a caring and supportive family that would help with his rehabilitation and reintegration into society. He echoed Shishir's point about conducting two separate trials but argued that both boys should be tried by the Juvenile Justice Board.

Soon after Haneef was arrested, neighbours forced his family to move out of their home. They have since been living in a rented flat but have filed a case in the Bombay High Court, asking that they be allowed to return to their home.

Even though Saif wasn't involved in Junera's kidnapping or murder, the police have charged him with both crimes, said his lawyer, Tahira Shaikh.[11] She alleged that the police had made up certain details to build their case and that Saif only came to know about Junera's murder when Haneef texted and asked him to come over.

She also said that the police didn't have any clue for fifteen days after Junera was reported missing. 'They added false details like the use of chloroform to add spice to their story for the media. No chloroform was found at the spot, nor did they submit a statement from the college saying that chloroform had been stolen from their laboratory. Even their sniffer dogs couldn't find anything,' she said.

Tahira added that owing to the poor quality of the police investigation, many aspects of the case may never be known. 'Apart from making one phone call to the girl's father, Saif had no involvement in the crime. A father lost his daughter and that is the most unfortunate thing. But we don't know the full story here. We still don't know how the girl died since her body was decomposed by the time it was found,' she said. She also said that she believed Haneef didn't intend to kill Junera and implied that her death may have been accidental.

According to Tahira, the police charge sheet alleged that Haneef and Saif had conspired to kill Junera, but they did

---

[11] From an interview with Tahira Shaikh in Mumbai on 15 March 2018.

not have a single piece of evidence for this claim. She also said that the two boys had known each other for only a few months prior to the crime.

The state's efforts to ensure that both the accused juveniles be tried as adults is still pending in the high court. Only after the resolution of these appeals can the actual trial of the case begin, where the prosecution will have to prove that Haneef and Saif are guilty. Until then, the fate of the two remains undecided.

* * *

In 2018, both Haneef and Saif appeared for their board exams—the former from the lock-up. Saif now plans to study medicine.

Mumtaz's life continues to revolve around the courts, and he is determined to get justice for Junera. 'The day I learnt that I had lost my daughter, I made a promise to myself that I would get justice for her. I will do everything in my power to make sure that Haneef and Saif are tried as adults,' he said.

Mumtaz recalls that on 5 December, while he was running helter-skelter in the neighbourhood looking for his daughter, Haneef had followed him around. 'He told me that he had asked the maulana of Kazipura Masjid to make an announcement about Junera's disappearance and offered to go to other mosques in the area as well. I was in a dazed state of mind and asked him to go ahead,' he said. Little did he know then that it was not an innocent offer of help.

Mumtaz often thinks about whether Haneef's parents tried to shield him from the police. He is fairly convinced that they knew nothing of Haneef's plans and had no role to play in any of it. Regardless, he cannot bear the thought of living in the same building as them.

Shahida and the other children, however, have tried hard to move on with their lives and rarely talk about Junera because it is too painful, Mumtaz said. Her sister, Muskaan, said, 'Junera loved to go to school with us and would often pose with her bag when we were at home, pretending she was ready for school.' After Junera's death, Mumtaz and Shahida had a son, whom they named Ghulam Mustafa.

Mumtaz never misses a court hearing and usually arrives an hour before the proceedings begin. But he is frustrated at the slow pace of the Indian judiciary. 'We were grateful that we had the support of the police and the general public. But attending the hearings is frustrating. Either the defence lawyer doesn't turn up or the hearing is postponed. The courts in our country really need more discipline so that parents like us won't have to wait years for justice,' he said.

To this day, despite the pain, Mumtaz often browses pictures of his daughter on his phone. 'She and I were very close. She loved cheese rolls and if I ever forgot to bring her one after work, I wouldn't hear the end of it. She was possessive of me and wouldn't allow anyone to touch my belongings. Every night after I returned from work, she would tell me everything that had happened that day,' he said, with tears welling up in his eyes. What keeps him going, he added, is the hope that Haneef and Saif will one day be held accountable, regardless of their age.

* * *

Every time there is a hearing either in the children's court, the juvenile justice court or at the Bombay High Court, Mumtaz is at the court well before the advocates of either party turn up. Every time, he fights the painful memories of that fateful night when he sees either Haneef or Saif waiting outside the courtroom.

Even though he knew very little about the system before, attending the hearings on a regular basis has taught him the ways of the court. Today, he has acquainted himself with the court staff and is always updated about the next hearing. A man who had never dealt with court proceedings before, over the course of a few weeks, can now effortlessly find his way around the court complex.

Unlike other parents who are present for the hearings but as silent spectators, Mumtaz is actively involved in the case. He regularly visits the state-appointed special public prosecutor Hirey's office to discuss the next course of action.

His determination to ensure that his daughter's killers are awarded the harshest sentence is admirable and endearing. While it lays bare the deep, unconditional love that they shared, Mumtaz has now taken the trial as a challenge. Anger is still visible on his face, and he will probably hold on to it till the very end.

Junera's story leaves behind a terrifying question for all parents. Is my child safe at home? It makes one wonder how far parents have to go to protect their children or loved ones from those who may cause them harm.

2

Ritesh and Mukta, Coimbatore

Young children seldom step out of their homes unaccompanied by an adult. But parents or family members can't be around their children at all times. Kidnappers know this too. In cases of kidnapping, most of the victims are either picked up when they're on their way to school or while returning back home.

The story of Ritesh and Mukta Jain[1] is one that most parents in Coimbatore are familiar with. Their brutal murder has made people more cautious and watchful of their children's movements.

***

Originally from Pali district in Rajasthan, the Jain family moved to Coimbatore in the 1950s. The second generation set up their home in a residential area at Kathan Chetty Lane. They had a handloom and hardware business of bath and

---

[1] Names have been changed since the case involves the rape of a minor girl.

furniture accessories. Eleven-year-old Mukta and seven-year-old Ritesh Jain studied in class VI and class III at Suguna Rip School, Tatabad, around 6 kilometres from their home.

Their parents, Rajan and Swati, had arranged for the children to be picked up by a school van run by a taxi company called Surya Cabs, which also picked up and dropped off other children in the neighbourhood. As the lane leading to their house was too narrow for the van, it would wait for Mukta and Ritesh on the main road, Rangai Gowder Street.

On 29 October 2010, Ritesh and Mukta were ready for school by 7.30 a.m. and left their house for the 500-metre walk down the lane to the pickup point. They were waiting in front of the Vinayak temple on the main road when a white Maruti Omni halted in front of them.

The person at the wheel, twenty-three-year-old Mohan Krishnan, was familiar to the children, but not their usual driver. There were no other children in the van—as there usually were—but neither thought much of it and got inside.

Instead of driving in the direction of the school, Mohan took the road to Pollachi, a town around 50 kilometres from Coimbatore.

When Mukta and Ritesh realized they were nowhere near their school, they began to panic. They repeatedly asked Mohan where he was taking them and begged to speak to their parents. Soon both were in tears.

To pacify the children, Mohan told them that he wasn't taking them to school but to a class picnic and assured them that all their friends were already there. The kids stopped crying and waited in silence.

Continuing on beyond Pollachi, Mohan stopped at his village of Angalakurichi. He and his parents had moved from there to Coimbatore seven years before in search of employment.

Here, Mohan picked up twenty-three-year-old R. Manoharan, his childhood friend and neighbour. Based on the confessions of the two men, the mahila court's judgment would later note that the two had chalked out their plan to kidnap the two children five days before abducting them.

To execute their plan, however, the two kidnappers needed money. Around 10 a.m., after picking up Manoharan, Mohan approached Senthil Kumar, who lived on the property owned by his family, and asked for that month's rent. Senthil, however, told him that he had already paid the rent to Mohan's mother. His plan foiled, Mohan returned to the van and drove off.

Though the kidnappers had a mobile phone, they chose not to use it to call the children's parents, knowing it would give away their location to the police.

'They knew that if they made the call from a mobile phone, the police would eventually track their location and find them. They had planned to demand a ransom of Rs 20 lakh. They decided to keep the children somewhere and make the ransom call from a landline,' said Thiru Kanagasabapathy, the investigating officer.[2]

After setting out from Angalakurichi, Mohan drove for another 30 kilometres towards the Western Ghats and stopped at the base of a hill. As soon as the van stopped, the children began to ask about their classmates. Mohan told them they were in the Gopalsamy temple atop the hill and told them to get out of the car.

Mohan and Manoharan were familiar with the area and knew there was no fixed path to the temple. To get there, they would have to trek through a forest with two frightened, unwilling children.

---

[2] From an interview with Thiru Kanagasabapathy in Coimbatore on 15 December 2017.

A. Annadurai, a member of the investigation team and inspector of the B-2 R.S. Puram police station at the time, said, 'They knew no one would be at the temple that day since devotees from villages nearby visited it only on Saturdays. They planned to hide the children there and call the parents for money.'

Reluctantly, Mukta and Ritesh began to climb the hill with their two captors. But 500 metres into their climb, the two exhausted children refused to go any farther. Mohan and Manoharan discussed their options and concluded that it would be nearly impossible to drag the two children, kicking and screaming, up the hill without anyone noticing. Thwarted again, they decided to return to the van. They forced the children inside and drove away.

They hadn't got far when the two kidnappers realized that while their dreams of a ransom were proving elusive, there was something they could have right now, if they wanted. Their attention turned to Mukta in the back seat.

Eight kilometres into their journey, Mohan parked the van in a mango orchard and he and Manoharan took turns raping the eleven-year-old girl. They forced Ritesh to sit in the front seat and each warned the boy not to turn around as the other assaulted her in the back of the van.

Investigating Officer Thiru said, 'Mukta was too young to understand what was happening to her. They warned the boy not to turn around as they took turns raping her. Mohan raped her first, while Manoharan kept an eye on the boy and hit him every time he tried to turn his head.' The post-mortem report would later note that Mukta suffered 'injuries to her vagina and anus due to forcible sexual assault'.[3]

---

[3] Mentioned in *The State vs R. Manoharan*, Sessions Case No. 44/2011 (Court of the Sessions Judge Magalir Neethimandram [Mahila Court], Coimbatore, 1 November 2012).

With their lust sated, the kidnappers—according to their retelling of events—realized the possible consequences of what they had done. No matter what happened now, they felt they could not return Mukta and Ritesh to their parents alive.

They drove back to Angalakurichi to clear their heads and figure out what to do next. After some deliberation, they decided to poison them with *sani* powder,[4] a toxic chemical used as an insecticide in parts of Tamil Nadu, which people mix with water and sprinkle in their courtyards. 'A number of suicide cases using sani powder have been reported in the state, and Mohan may have heard about them. They decided to mix the powder with milk and feed it to the children.

---

[4] Sani is the Tamil word for cow dung. According to a research paper published by Dr Avinash and Dr Navin Puttum of the department of emergency medicine of Vinayaka Mission Kirupananda Variyar Medical College Hospital in Salem, cow dung was traditionally used as a germicide and insect repellent in homes, courtyards and temples in Tamil Nadu. The sani powder available these days, however, has little in common with cow dung. It is made, instead, with two deadly and therefore banned toxins called Auromine and Malachite Green.

Despite being banned, sani powder is cheap and readily available in Tamil Nadu and continues to be used as an insecticide in homes and temples. Ingesting it can kill a person in as little as a few hours, and many deaths, including suicides, reported in the state have been attributed to the toxin. It causes severe liver damage and can lead to full liver failure. In many of the cases reported in the state, the person died on the first day itself.

'All the patients with a history of ingestion of sani powder who reported to the Vinayaka Mission Kirupananda Variyar Medical College Hospital in Salem had severe liver dysfunction and derangement of coagulation. The illegal sale and mostly suicidal ingestion of sani powder are prevalent in the rural areas irrespective of strict legal measures.' See http://www.ijsrp.org/research-paper-0916/ijsrp-p5715.pdf.

Once they fell unconscious, they would leave their bodies in a forest,' said Thiru.

It was around 12.30 p.m. by the time Mohan and Manoharan drove back to their village and bought a packet of sani powder. They also bought some milk from a tea stall. Many eyewitnesses would later testify that they saw the two children sitting in the back of the van. Among them was B. Sarvanakumar, the owner of the tea stall, who knew both the men.

Sarvanakumar later told the police that he had asked Mohan and Manoharan about the two children, and Mohan had said they were taking them to a school picnic. The two men finished their tea and left soon after, he recalled.

Mohan and Manoharan drove the van another 15 kilometres to Mithiparai in Tirupur district. After parking at a secluded spot, the two men mixed the sani powder with milk in a plastic tumbler and forced the kids to drink it. Petrified, they obeyed and drank a little but found the taste unpleasant and refused to drink any more. The post-mortem report would later confirm the presence of the chemical in the small intestines of both children, but the dose wasn't lethal.

Mohan and Manoharan knew that it wouldn't be enough to kill them. Frustrated, they returned to Angalakurichi to figure out another way of killing them.

About an hour later, the van with all four headed towards the Parambikulam Aliyar Project (PAP) canal about 70 kilometres away. Mohan and Manoharan had decided that drowning the children was the best option at hand.

Mohan stopped the van at Deepalapatti, close to the massive canal. The canal was very deep, and people living in the area knew that the current was too strong for anyone to swim in it. They thought that if they pushed the children into the canal, their bodies would travel at least 100–150 kilometres and that there was a good chance they would never be found,' said Annadurai.[5]

They told the children to eat the lunch they had brought from home. When they finished eating, around 3.30 p.m., the two men told them to go wash their hands in the canal.

Annadurai said, 'While Mukta went towards the water, Ritesh was reluctant to go. Mohan grabbed him by his neck and dragged him before pushing both of them into the canal.' The two men walked another 500 metres and threw the children's school bags and lunch boxes in as well before returning to the van.

Mohan dropped Manoharan to his house, and a few hours later was back in Coimbatore, where the Jains were engaged in a frantic search for their missing children. It hadn't taken long for the family to realize that Mukta and Ritesh had vanished. Just ten minutes after Mohan picked them up in his van, the regular school van had arrived outside their lane. As there was no sign of the children, the driver telephoned their mother, Swati.[6] Seconds into the conversation, Swati realized that something terrible had happened.

Accompanied by Vijay, one of her three brothers-in-law who lived in the same house, she went out to look for her children. They first went to the children's school, just in case they had taken a ride with someone else. By the time they arrived, the morning prayer had already begun. When it ended, they approached the principal to ask if Ritesh and Mukta had made it to school.

---

[5] From an interview with A. Annadurai in Coimbatore on 18 December 2017.

[6] Name changed since the case involves the rape of a minor girl.

The principal immediately summoned a teacher, who confirmed their worst fears—neither child was in class. Vijay said, 'The principal issued directions to search all the classrooms. They also searched the prayer hall and the school grounds but they were nowhere to be found.'[7]

Vijay decided it was time to approach the police, and the two went to B-8 Variety Hall police station. The police registered their complaint at 9.40 a.m. Inspector Thiru accompanied them to their house.

When Vijay, Swati and the inspector arrived, there was already a large crowd of anxious relatives outside their home. Swati's husband, Rajan,[8] however, was in Hyderabad for work. Surrounded by his brothers, she told her husband the horrifying news.

Her three brothers-in-law then decided to form groups to search different parts of the city for Mukta and Ritesh. 'I wasn't ready to accept that they had been kidnapped. We looked for them everywhere we could think of—railway stations, bus depots, parks and around their school,' said Vijay.

Meanwhile, Inspector Thiru began to question the family's neighbours and relatives. Soon enough, he had his first big clue. Kasturibai, the children's grandmother, told him that she had seen the children enter what she had assumed was their school van. The case was now clearly one of kidnapping.

The inspector asked if she knew the identity of the driver. She didn't know his name but had seen him picking up the children for school around six months ago. She may not have

---

[7] From an interview with Vijay Jain in Coimbatore on 16 December 2017.

[8] Name changed since the case involves the rape of a minor girl.

been able to reveal the kidnapper's identity, but Kasturibai had given Inspector Thiru an important clue—the children knew their kidnapper well enough to get into his van.

Thiru said, 'The grandmother was confused when her relatives filled her in on what had happened. She dismissed what her relatives told her, insisting that she had seen the school van pick the children up. After speaking to her, we realized that the driver must have been someone the children knew.'

Next, the police got in touch with P. Karthikeyan, the owner of Surya Cabs, and asked for a list of all the drivers who had worked for them in the past two years. They soon received a list of five people. Four of them could be found easily. The fifth, a twenty-three-year-old named Mohan, was missing.

All four drivers were summoned to the police station for questioning. One of them, A. Anbu, told the police that Mohan had borrowed the Maruti Omni van he had been driving, saying he needed to take his wife to the temple. He said Mohan had promised to bring it back in an hour but hadn't returned yet and had even stopped answering his calls.

The police soon learnt that Mohan had joined Surya Cabs at the end of May. Once, when Karthikeyan asked him to pick up schoolchildren for a picnic, Mohan had collected Rs 500 from some of the parents. Karthikeyan soon found out about this and fired Mohan, just twenty days after he had joined.

By now the police were almost certain that Mohan was their prime suspect, and their theory was validated when they showed Kasturibai a photograph of him. She immediately confirmed that he was the man she had seen picking up her two grandchildren that morning.

After confirming his identity, however, the police said that they did not visit his house in Kovanoor where he stayed with his parents or his house in Angalakurichi. When asked for a reason, Thiru said that they didn't want to risk alerting Mohan.

But the police had another problem to overcome. Around noon, fed up with Anbu's incessant calls, Mohan had switched off his phone.

After speaking to the police, Anbu tried calling Mohan's mobile phone again. At 2.30 p.m., his persistence was rewarded when Manoharan picked up the phone. He told Anbu they were on their way back and switched the phone off again. The next call came around 4 p.m. This time Mohan was on the line, saying he would bring the van back in an hour.

The police decided they would wait for the kidnappers to return. To avoid spooking them, they sent Anbu alone to his house but were in constant touch with him for any updates on Mohan's whereabouts. At the time Mohan made the last call, the police said that he was at least 40 kilometres away from Anbu's house. He dropped Manoharan off at Angalakurichi on the way back and continued to drive towards Coimbatore. Around 8 p.m., Mohan called Anbu to tell him that he was on his way back, and an hour later parked the van in front of his house.

Anbu checked the odometer and calculated that Mohan had driven more than 250 kilometres that day. He asked him where he had gone and what he had done. Mohan confided in Anbu and began to tell him what he and Manoharan had done that day.

When he found an opportunity, Anbu called the police and informed them that Mohan had arrived at his house with the van. The police rushed to his house and got there at 9.45 p.m., just in time to catch Mohan as he was about to leave.

It wasn't long before the police pieced together what the two men had done in those twelve hours. When they looked into the van, they found a pair of pink panties under the seat and a yellow stain on the floor mat, which was later identified as sani powder in the forensic tests. The police noted that the panties had several strands of pubic hair. A DNA test revealed that the hair strands belonged to Manoharan.

Shortly after his arrest, Mohan confessed that he and Manoharan had kidnapped the children, raped Mukta and then pushed them into the PAP canal. While questioning Mohan's and Manoharan's family members, the police found out that the two had gone to the same school and remained close friends over the years. Mohan had studied up to class VIII while Manoharan had dropped out after class V. Thiru added that the police had no idea that Mohan had an accomplice until he told them about Manoharan's involvement.

On 30 October, a team of six policemen travelled to Manoharan's village but couldn't find him at his house. They searched for him the entire day before finally arresting him at 7.15 a.m. the next day. 'Many villagers had seen him around the government school nearby. We found him hiding behind a bush. He had been following the story on news channels and knew we would eventually come for him. When we arrested him, he didn't even try to escape,' said Thiru.

Annadurai said the police soon noticed yellow stains on his hands, a sign that he may have handled the sani powder. 'According to Mohan's confession, Manoharan had mixed the powder in milk. This powder tends to leave a yellow stain, which takes three to four days to fade away. When we questioned Manoharan, he initially denied he had done anything, but later confessed,' said Annadurai.

Medical reports prepared by a doctor at a government hospital also noted contusions on the genital organ/penis of both Mohan and Manoharan.

* * *

But the police still had another important job to do—find the bodies of the children. 'Even though we had found Mohan and he had confessed to having kidnapped and murdered them, it wouldn't have been enough unless we found the bodies,' said Thiru. The search for Mukta's and Ritesh's bodies involved seventy-five policemen from Coimbatore and Tirupur. They spent the night of 29 October and the next day scouring the entire length of the canal.

Mukta's body was the first to be found. N. Sathish, a passer-by, saw the girl's body on the bank of the canal at Palladam around 10 a.m. on 30 October. The area was around 70 kilometres from where she had been pushed into the canal.

Sathish pulled her body on to dry land.

They still had to find Ritesh's body. After searching for a few more hours, the police decided that drastic measures were needed. They asked the authorities concerned to reduce the flow of water from Thirumoorthy Malai dam for some time. They did so, and about six hours later, Ritesh's body was found in a section of the canal around 500 metres from the road from Pollachi to Udumalpet Highway, in an area called Kedimedu. Ritesh's body had travelled only 14 kilometres as it had become entangled in some thorny bushes, according to Annadurai.

He added that the boy's post-mortem report had revealed that his hyoid bone—otherwise known as the tongue bone—

had been fractured, suggesting that Mohan had dragged him to the edge of the canal by his throat.

After locating the children's bodies, the police investigation now focused on collecting material evidence and finding witnesses. Thiru, while going over the details of Mohan's confession, realized that the plastic tumbler they had used to mix the sani powder with milk at Mithiparai village would be an important piece of evidence.

On 8 November, the judicial magistrate placed Mohan and Manoharan in police custody for three days, after which Thiru and his team decided to take them to collect evidence along the route they had taken on the day they kidnapped and killed the two children. After police custody was granted, they kept Mohan and Manoharan at the Saravanampatti police station with five inspectors and five special inspectors in charge of both of them.

Though cases of kidnapping are fairly common in Coimbatore, the police claim that this case, where the kidnappers were faced with charges of kidnapping, rape and murder, was the first of its kind. 'After their arrest, there was a lot of pressure from the public, demanding justice, and the media, which demanded more information. Apart from the flood of questions, we had to keep the very angry public away from the accused, who would have otherwise killed them,' said Thiru.

To keep them away from the public eye, the police planned to recover the evidence and return to Coimbatore before 9 a.m. on 9 November. At 5 a.m., the police set out for Pollachi with Mohan and Manoharan in two separate vans. Thiru was in the first van with Manoharan, and Annadurai followed in the second van with Mohan, accompanied by Sub-Inspectors T. Jothy and S. Muthumalai, among others.

Though both the vehicles left at the same time, the van in which Thiru was travelling was soon a couple of kilometres ahead of the second one. After travelling for about 10 kilometres, the second van reached the railway gate at Eachanari, which was blocked. Annadurai called Thiru to ask about the route they had taken. Following Thiru's instructions, Annadurai gave directions to the driver to take the road towards Podanur in Chettipalayam.

Recalling the seating arrangement in the Eicher van, which has a capacity of twenty people, Annadurai said, 'I sat in front of Mohan on the left side of the van while Jothi sat in the seat adjacent to him with Muthumalai behind him. Two other constables sat behind Mohan and all of us had weapons.' Annadurai and Muthumalai had a 9 mm pistol each, and Jothi had a revolver.

According to Annadurai, around 5.45 a.m., when the second van crossed Podanur, Mohan shouted and snatched Jothi's revolver. He pointed it at the policemen inside the van and yelled at the driver to divert the vehicle towards Palakkad in Kerala, where his family hailed from.

Annadurai, Jothi and Muthumalai tried to calm him down and get him to return the revolver. In return, they only got abuses like 'police naai' (police are dogs) from Mohan. 'As we were trying to convince him to hand over the gun, he fired. He shot Jothi in his left upper arm and Muthumalai on the left side of the abdomen. Acting in self-defence, Muthumalai fired two shots, while I fired one, and within seconds Mohan collapsed,' said Annadurai. Mohan was shot twice in the head and once in the chest, and died on the spot.

The police van rushed to the Government Medical College Hospital in Coimbatore, around 15 kilometres from

Podanur. In the meantime, Annadurai called the police control room and informed the senior police officers about the incident. The two policemen survived and were later shifted to a private hospital.

Various newspapers reported that when the news of the encounter spread on television channels, people rejoiced and celebrated with firecrackers and sweets.[9] While people were visibly elated about Mohan's death, there were reports that suggested that the encounter was staged to assuage the growing outrage of the public.

Nonetheless, Mohan was additionally charged, after his death, with attempted murder, attempt to escape from police custody and handling a firearm without a licence.

Thiru didn't hear from Annadurai until he reached Pollachi with Manoharan. After being told about Mohan's death, he took Manoharan to the Pollachi police station and called his senior officers for further directions. 'After some time, I was instructed to complete the investigation and return with Manoharan as soon as possible. I took him to Mithiparai village, and he showed us where he had thrown the disposable cup. I then returned to Coimbatore,' said Thiru.

Even though much of the planning was done by Mohan, he had found a willing partner in Manoharan. During the investigation, Annadurai found out that while Mohan's father was a driver, Manoharan's parents were daily-wage workers. According to Mohan's confession, initially, a ransom of

---

9   http://epaper.timesofindia.com/Repository/getFiles. asp?Style=OliveXLib:LowLevelEntityToPrint_TOI&Type=text/ html&Locale=english-skin-custom&Path=TOIKM/2010/11/10& ID=Ar00108

around Rs 20 lakh was the only motive behind kidnapping the children.

Annadurai also came to know that Mohan had been planning to kidnap the two children for nearly a month before he decided to go through with it. After Karthikeyan fired him from Surya Cabs in June that year, he had taken up a short-term job as a driver.

Mohan had long wanted to purchase taxis of his own to start a business that would solve his financial troubles. During this time, he met three other drivers who shared his ambition.

'Around twenty-five days before the incident, he shared his plan to kidnap Mukta and Ritesh with the other three drivers, who at the time agreed to participate. They were convinced that kidnapping was the only way to get such a large sum of money as ransom. However, on the day, after Mohan arranged for the van, they all backed out. But he decided to go ahead with his plan with Manoharan instead,' said Annadurai. Two of those drivers, N. Jayakumar and S. Apsal, later mentioned it in their official statements as witnesses.

Since the case involved the rape and murder of children, the state government appointed V. Sankaranarayanan as the special public prosecutor, who represented the state in the Madras High Court as well. Even with fifty-two years' experience, Sankaranarayanan admitted that a case involving kidnapping, rape and murder was rare.[10]

Even though there were no witnesses who saw Mohan and Manoharan kidnap, rape or murder the children, Sankaranarayanan felt that the police had abundant circumstantial evidence, including medical evidence, which

---

[10] From an interview with U. Sankaranarayanan in Coimbatore on 16 December 2017.

helped them present a strong case. Right from the beginning of the trial, Sankaranarayanan had demanded a death sentence for Manoharan and was thus satisfied with the judgment.

Throughout the trial, Manoharan's advocate maintained the stand that he was a silent spectator and had no role to play in the kidnapping of the children. Sankaranarayanan countered this by saying that since Mohan had died in the encounter, Manoharan was simply trying to shift all the blame on his associate. 'Apart from all the medical evidence, at the time of the police interrogation, he had confessed to being an equal participant in all that had happened. But during the trial, he changed his stand. In all of my interactions, I never felt that Manoharan seemed repentant,' Sankaranarayanan said.

He recalled how shattered the parents seemed when they appeared in court to give their statements. During one of the hearings, the children's mother, Swati, was unable to open her mouth when Sankaranarayanan tried to ask her some questions. 'She had lost both her children in a single day. I tried to give her strength to urge her to speak but she couldn't and broke down. I realized that she wouldn't be able to continue and when I turned around, I noticed that everyone in the courtroom was crying,' he said.

Two years after Ritesh and Mukta were kidnapped and murdered, the mahila court found Manoharan guilty of murder, rape, kidnapping for ransom and criminal conspiracy. On 1 November 2012 the sessions court judge Magalir Neethimandram sentenced him to death.[11]

---

[11] *The State vs R. Manoharan*, Sessions Case No. 44/2011 (Court of the Sessions Judge Magalir Neethimandram [Mahila Court], Coimbatore, 1 November 2012).

Manoharan's lawyer appealed against the judgment in the Madras High Court, which upheld his death sentence on 24 March 2014. The case was then presented before the Supreme Court and a stay order was granted on the death sentence on 13 October 2014. The final judgment in the case is still awaited.

On the day the judgment was pronounced at the mahila court in Coimbatore, thousands of people from Coimbatore and neighbouring areas turned up at the court. After they found out about the death sentence awarded to Manoharan, they distributed sweets among themselves. Sankaranarayanan pointed out that the parents, however, did not come to court. Owing to their religious identity, they were praying in the Jain temple since they didn't want a death sentence for Manoharan.[12]

Such was the public outcry over the crimes that the Coimbatore bar council refused to represent Manoharan and passed a resolution to that effect. Because of this, the legal aid cell was his only recourse. The first four advocates appointed to defend him refused to do so. Some newspapers claimed that they withdrew due to the heinous nature of the crime committed by the two of them.[13]

Finally, the fifth advocate appointed to represent Manoharan, A. Sharmila, chose to put duty first. It wasn't an easy decision. At one point, the district judge even offered her

---

[12] Jainism follows the supreme principle of non-violence. Its theology teaches that one must not kill another living being nor cause another to kill, nor consent to any killing directly or indirectly.

[13] https://timesofindia.indiatimes.com/city/coimbatore/Final-argument-in-Jain-siblings-murder-trial-to-be-heard-on-Oct-22/articleshow/16831635.cms

police protection, which she declined. 'Some of my colleagues asked me why I took up the case. But as an advocate, it is my job to argue for Manoharan just as a doctor has to treat a patient regardless of who he or she is,' she said.[14]

She argued that there was no medical evidence to prove that Manoharan had committed rape. She maintained that Manoharan, who had no past criminal record, was with the children for only a part of the journey in the van. 'He was dropped off at the Mariamma temple in Pollachi, and he didn't sexually assault Mukta. The police planted his DNA in the van to frame him. What happened to the children was unfortunate but the police have caught the wrong person,' she said.

Pointing out other anomalies in the evidence, she said that the children's father, Rajan, who had identified the panties found in the van, was in Hyderabad on the day of the incident and couldn't have known what the undergarment his daughter was wearing looked like.

She further contended that none of the eyewitnesses who claimed to have seen the four of them together had said that the children looked distressed or scared at any point of time, which could have led them to suspect that something was amiss. She also alleged that the witnesses had been tutored by the police to support the stand mentioned in the charge sheet.

Recalling the day of the judgment, she said that apart from the media putting pressure on the judges, there were also twenty young girls sitting in the courtroom that day—possibly to influence the judge.

---

[14] From an interview with A. Sharmila in Coimbatore on 18 December 2017.

She described Manoharan as a well-behaved person. 'He converted to Christianity after he was taken into judicial custody and still has hopes from the judicial system. He maintains that he is innocent. He is well mannered and there have been no complaints about him in jail,' she said.

When asked, she said that she believed the theory that Mohan had been killed by the police in a fake encounter because of the public outrage over the crimes, and added that Manoharan would have had a better chance of proving his innocence had Mohan been alive.

* * *

For Mukta and Ritesh's parents, neither Mohan's death nor Manoharan's death sentence has made the pain of losing their children any more bearable. Memories of their playful son and ambitious daughter haunt them even today. 'Mukta was a studious child, always interested in learning new things. She aspired to become an IAS officer when she grew up. Since we lived in a joint family, we were all very close and we miss them all the time, but especially on their birthdays,' said their uncle Vijay, fighting back tears.

After the incident occurred and throughout the trial, the family received a lot of support from people in the city and beyond. Around 20,000 people attended the funeral procession held on 31 October 2010. Vijay said that no one in the area celebrated Diwali that year, which was just a week after the incident.

Vijay recalled that the general public displayed more anger against the accused than any of the family members. During the trial, the police faced great difficulty in bringing the accused to the court since the public threw potatoes and eggs to show their anger. Vijay felt that, like the Jain family, people in Coimbatore too had pinned their hopes on the legal system.

Even though the entire family tried to help the inconsolable parents cope with the loss of their children, it wasn't easy. Understandably, it was difficult for Rajan to focus on work after losing both his children. 'After a point, he wanted to forget all of it and move on. But it's hard to escape from it all. Even in the shop, someone would bring up the topic of the children. It took him about a year and a half to start working again,' said Vijay.

But Rajan and his wife were determined to move on. In December 2017, Swati gave birth to a baby boy. When asked if the family was considering moving elsewhere, Vijay said that they wouldn't even think about it due to the immense support the people of the city had showed towards their family, including political parties and the police.

After the incident, the family, which has five other children in the house, decided to take up certain safety measures, as did four of their neighbours. They installed CCTV cameras and fortified their gates. For a few days after the incident, the children in their neighbourhood were not allowed to step out of the house unless accompanied by an adult.

The family members were grateful that the trial had been taken up expeditiously and the verdict pronounced in two years' time. 'We got the confidence to continue because of the immense support we received from people. The public support we saw wasn't just for Ritesh and Mukta; it was for all their children as well. Our family members are not the only ones who are involved in this case. The people living in this city are also an equal part of it,' said Vijay. The family now hopes that the Supreme Court will give Manoharan the punishment he rightfully deserves.

* * *

Coimbatore has the feel of a sleepy little town, and women generally feel safe enough to use public transportation at night. Even though the police deal with cases involving serious offences like murder on a regular basis, Ritesh and Mukta's case is one of a kind. It came as a jolt to the police as well as the public at the time.

Everyone involved in the case, right from the investigating officer to the advocate representing the state, remembered every detail of the case without the help of any documents.

The ease with which Mukta and Ritesh were kidnapped while they were walking to the bus stop forces one to think about the ways in which a very regular day could turn into something so tragic.

The unimaginable agony their parents must still be going through is the reason why they are extremely reluctant to talk about the case with anyone, family or otherwise.

It is spine-chilling to even imagine how petrified Mukta and Ritesh must have been in their last moments. A regular day that should have been spent in school followed by tuition classes ended in a manner so horrific that even the police struggled to find the appropriate words to describe the details accurately.

The birth of their son is a new beginning for the entire Jain family. Rajan and Swati's life is a lesson on how to live with the worst memories and yet learn to move on in order to make new ones.

3

Tanya Patel, Nadiad

Tanya Patel was a shy class II student at S.N.V. International School at Nadiad in Gujarat. The daughter of Amit Kumar Patel and his wife, Gayatri, she was brought up by her grandparents. Amit and Gayatri married in 2009 and decided to emigrate to the UK. When Tanya was born a year later, they felt they wouldn't be able to take good care of her due to their long working hours. They decided to leave her in the care of her maternal grandparents, hoping they would be able to provide the child a stable environment.

After three years at her maternal grandparents' house, Tanya was then taken in by her paternal grandmother, Kusumben Patel, to whom she became deeply attached.[1] Kusumben was the principal of a school in Sihunj, 17 kilometres from Nadiad, a small town around 70 kilometres away from Ahmedabad. When she retired, around two and a half years later, they moved into a new home at Laksh Duplex Society near the

---

[1]   From an interview with Kusumben Patel in Nadiad on 25 January 2018.

Santram Mandir in Nadiad, located near the subsections of a canal and home to members of the Patel community.

Since Tanya had not lived with her parents for most of her life, she was close to her grandparents. They ensured that Tanya never missed out on any experience because of her parents' absence. While other parents took their children to birthday parties, Kusumben would take Tanya herself or send her with a reliable parent.

On 11 September 2017, Tanya turned seven and Kusumben organized a party for her granddaughter. Among the guests were their neighbours—forty-one-year-old Jigisha Patel, her sons, Meet, twenty-two, and Dhruv, nineteen, and the family's domestic help, seventeen-year-old Vijay.[2] Jigisha's family had moved into Laksh Duplex society about a year and a half earlier and Kusumben had known her well for about a year. Everyone sang along as Tanya cut her birthday cake and Kusumben recalls that Jigisha gave Tanya a 100-rupee note before leaving.

A week later, on 18 September, Tanya left for school around 7 a.m. and returned at 3 p.m. After feeding her, Kusumben took her to her tuition class around 4.45 p.m. They returned home by 6.30 p.m. A disciplined woman, Kusumben made it a point to eat dinner early. Half an hour later she sat down with her granddaughter for a meal of saag, rotis and milk.

While they were eating, Jigisha rang the doorbell and asked for some onions, which Kusumben gave her. After dinner, Tanya asked if she could go play with her friend Bittu Patel, who lived next door and was a year older than her. Like any doting grandmother, Kusumben rarely refused Tanya

---

[2] Name changed since he is a juvenile accused.

anything. She dressed her up and watched her leave the house before turning her attention to the unwashed dishes.

When Tanya went next door, however, Bittu's mother refused to let them play and asked Tanya to go back home. As she turned around, Tanya saw Anjuben Patel, another neighbour, sitting on a cot in the common area between the flats and sat down with her.

Kusumben, who was unaware of all this at the time, was later told by the police that while Tanya was sitting with Anju, Jigisha came out of her house and asked Anju to get a candle from her house. 'By that time, Meet had arrived in a white Hyundai i10 which he parked near the gate. At 7.45 p.m., when Anju went back inside, Jigisha told Tanya that Meet was waiting for her in the car,' Kusumben said. The police also said that after taking Tanya to the car, Jigisha went back inside to avoid being seen.

When she got into the car, Meet, whom Tanya called Meet kaka (uncle), told her they were going to get some ice cream. The car did not belong to him. He had borrowed it from a friend, saying he needed to take his family to the Ambaji temple in Banaskantha, about 50 kilometres from his home.

A few minutes later, Meet allegedly picked up his accomplice Vijay. He then drove 20 kilometres and stopped at a Havmor ice-cream stall in Vidyanagar, where he bought Tanya the treat he had promised her. He then drove for another 25 kilometres until they reached the Vasad bridge, which spans the Mahi River.

Meet got out of the car and asked Tanya to follow. She was reluctant at first and asked Meet to take her back home, but he insisted. He asked her again and sat down on the footpath near the 2.5-foot-tall iron grille that ran along the boundary of the bridge.

Tanya got out of the car, walked to the footpath and sat down next to Meet. That was the cue. Meet and Vijay allegedly picked her up and threw her off the bridge.

Dhirubhai Baldaniya, the investigating officer of the case, said, 'He lured her to come near the edge of the bridge under the pretext of showing her fish in the river. Once she went close enough, the two of them threw her into the river.'[3] Recalling what the police later told her, Kusumben, fighting back tears, said that Tanya had told Meet several times during the journey that she was sleepy and wanted to go back home to her grandmother.

Meet and Vijay quickly got back into the car, turned it around and sped back home at a speed of 120–130 kilometres per hour, as they did not want to risk anyone noticing that they were not at home.

* * *

Back at Laksh Duplex society, Kusumben was done washing the dishes. At 8.10 p.m., she stepped out of her home and rested on the cot in the common area. Jigisha brought a chair from her house to sit with her and the two spoke for about fifteen minutes before Kusumben decided it was time for Tanya to go to bed. She called out for her granddaughter.

She didn't get a response, so Kusumben walked over to Bittu's house. She called out to Bittu who came to the front door alone a few seconds later. Kusumben broke into full-

---

[3] From an interview with Dhirubhai Baldaniya in Nadiad on 24 January 2018.

blown panic when Bittu told her she didn't know where Tanya was.

Her mind clouded with fear and confusion, Kusumben began looking for her missing granddaughter everywhere. She knocked on every door in the society, and word of Tanya's disappearance spread quickly. Kusumben knew one thing. Her granddaughter was terrified of the dark and couldn't possibly have walked out all by herself. She began to suspect that if Tanya had left the society, it had been with a known person.

Kusumben did her best to suppress her fear. Convincing herself that Tanya was all right and would be found soon, she decided she wouldn't tell her son about his daughter's disappearance just yet. But once others in the society knew what had happened, word spread like wildfire on social media, and in a few hours Tanya's parents got to know of her disappearance from one of their relatives.

Tanya's maternal grandfather, Bhaubhai Ambala Puri, remembered a similar experience a few months before. 'Around six months ago, Tanya didn't get off the school bus. After frantic phone calls from Kusumben, the driver found her asleep in the bus. I hoped that something like that had happened again. I didn't want to believe otherwise,' said Bhaubhai.

Meanwhile, Meet and Vijay had returned home. Barely an hour after allegedly pushing the seven-year-old girl to her death, they joined in the search for her with the other neighbours to avert suspicion. But with Tanya nowhere to be found, Kusumben finally decided to go to the police.

Around 9.30 p.m., a group of people accompanied her to Nadiad West police station at Vallabh Nagar, including her relative Devyani Patel and her family, who lived in the same society.[4] Meet also tagged along with them.

The police registered a case of kidnapping and sent out a search team for the missing girl, unaware that Tanya had been dead for more than an hour.

Over the next two days, around 150 policemen, including those from the rural police, town police and other police stations in the area, searched the society and various large agricultural plots around it for clues. They deployed a drone to search the areas around the canal that ran along the society while divers looked for clues underwater.

The atmosphere was fraught with anxiety and few in the neighbourhood slept on the night of 18 September. While everyone else was wondering how Tanya, who never left the house without her grandmother, had vanished, Meet and his mother, Jigisha, seemed more interested in the progress of the police investigation. It wasn't long before their behaviour caught the attention of Dhirubhai and Inspector Vikram Singh Rathod from the local crime branch.[5]

Recalling the day after Tanya went missing, Dhirubhai said that while Tanya's relatives, neighbours and family friends sat together near Kusumben's house, Meet would sit with the police or follow them around to overhear their conversations about the investigation. 'He constantly tried to offer us help, but in reality, he just wanted to keep tabs on our movements. His mother, Jigisha, sat with the policewomen and tried to get information from them. From time to time she pretended to shed tears,' said Dhirubhai . Meet's brother, Dhruv, on the other hand, tried to not attract any attention by staying indoors and didn't leave the neighbourhood at all.

Many journalists who interviewed Tanya's relatives also recalled Meet's odd behaviour. Dhruti Dave Mistry, a news reporter who followed the case closely, said, 'While the relatives kept to themselves, he would constantly be around us, asking if the police had said anything or if we had any updates about Tanya. He seemed quite edgy and I strongly felt something about his behaviour was suspicious.'

As Rathod questioned members of Tanya's family and her neighbours, it became clear to him as well that it was highly unlikely that the seven-year-old had left the society on her own. It seemed much more plausible that she had left with someone she knew well. Given his experience with such cases, Rathod knew the three most likely motives behind kidnapping cases were ransom, revenge or rape.

He and his team members checked the backgrounds of all the young, single men who lived in the society. Among these was Meet, whose wife had left him a few months after their wedding, and seventeen-year-old Vijay, his domestic help. The investigation revealed that Meet's family was in financial trouble. Neither he nor his father had had a job in a long time. The first red flag.

Undeterred by the swarm of policemen around their house, Meet and his accomplices—Jigisha, Dhruv and Vijay—decided to go ahead with the next part of their plan. For this they roped in Kunal,[6] a sixteen-year-old boy who was a part of Meet's friend circle. Meet told Kunal to meet him at

---

[6] Name changed since he is a juvenile accused.

their usual hang-out spot near the canal. Once he got there, he filled him in about Tanya's kidnapping.

Kunal reportedly later told the police that Meet had asked him to go to Baroda and make a ransom call to Kusumben's phone. The police explained that when a kidnapping victim's family receives a ransom call, the first step is to track the location of the caller. Meet thought that if the call came from another city, it would throw the police investigation off track.

It took some convincing but Kunal decided to get involved when Meet told him about the phone conversations between Kusumben and her son who lived in the UK. Dhirubhai said, 'Kusumben's house lacked network coverage so she had a habit of stepping out to answer phone calls. She often discussed financial matters with her son, including details of the money he would send her. Meet and his mother had overheard quite a few of these conversations and knew that Kusumben had money.' As per their plan, Meet instructed Kunal to demand a ransom of Rs 18 lakh, saying that his cut would be Rs 3 lakh. Kunal agreed and left on his motorbike for Baroda, around 60 kilometres away.

But Meet's confidence turned out to be short-lived when he saw more policemen joining the investigation. He realized that a ransom call at that point would only increase his chances of being caught and decided to call off the plan. He called Kunal around 1 p.m. to ask him not to make the ransom call and to return to Nadiad.

While the police continued to look for clues about Tanya's whereabouts, Meet tried his best to throw them off the scent. Dhirubhai said Meet told the police he may have seen Tanya walking towards Prima Flora, where she went for tuitions, and urged them to check the CCTV camera footage from the area.

Another senior police official, who did not wish to be named, said that since the Patels are a close-knit community, no one suspected 'one of their own' could have kidnapped Tanya. He said that while the police were searching for her, a misleading post on Instagram was being spread by members of the Patel community which included a picture of Tanya with a message indicating that she had been found and was fine. The police later suspected that Meet had created the post to mislead the police, though they found no evidence to back this claim.

Two days passed and the police's hope of finding Tanya alive started to dwindle. As their search continued, Dhirubhai noticed that apart from Meet and Vijay, Kunal too would trail the policemen wherever they went. To test this, Dhirubhai walked to the area behind the society, near the canal. He turned around and sure enough saw Kunal following him.

The police felt that their suspicion about Meet, Vijay and Kunal was strong enough to call them in for questioning. On 21 September, they were picked up by the police separately. While Dhirubhai interrogated Kunal, Rathod questioned Meet and Vijay.

The police's initial line of questioning was met with nothing but vehement denials from Kunal, who seemed determined not to give anything away. When asked about Tanya's disappearance, he maintained that he knew nothing. Dhirubhai then asked him why he was following the police. Kunal denied this, insisting that he frequented the area near the canal and had only gone there to smoke a cigarette.

But according to the police, after a three-hour interrogation, in which they used various tactics to get Kunal to talk, he admitted he knew Tanya's kidnappers. He eventually told them that Meet had sent him to Nadiad to make a ransom call before getting cold feet and calling him back.

In order to cajole him to reveal what else he knew, the police promised to spare him if he hadn't done anything. Dhirubhai said that Kunal probably confessed relatively quickly because of his limited involvement in Tanya's kidnap and murder.

After obtaining Kunal's confession, the police increased the pressure on Meet and Vijay who were seated in another room. Meet denied knowing anything and maintained that he was at home when Tanya went missing. With Kunal having confessed everything, the police had no intention of letting Meet and Vijay go. They continued the interrogation, hoping to catch Meet in his lies. It wasn't long before Meet reportedly admitted to the police that he had kidnapped the seven-year-old girl and thrown her off Vasad bridge. Vijay confessed as well, but said he had acted on Meet's directions.

The kidnappers told the police chilling details of their plan and revealed that they had intended to kill Tanya from the start. According to Dhirubhai, Meet and members of his family had been planning the kidnap and murder since 16 September and had spent a lot of time thinking about the best way to dispose of Tanya's body. Reasoning that someone could find her if they simply threw her body into the river, they came up with a plan—to weigh her body down with a rock. But for this, Meet would have to kill or incapacitate her first.

According to Dhirubhai, Meet and Vijay had placed a large rock in the car before taking Tanya to Vasad bridge but didn't end up using it and left it near the canal. The police later escorted Meet to the area and recovered the rock.

After the police told her that Meet and his relatives had kidnapped and killed Tanya, Kusumben recalled—and began to make sense of—their behaviour the night she disappeared. 'Even after I looked everywhere and couldn't find Tanya, I thought it would be best to inform the police. But Jigisha kept dissuading me from doing so. She insisted that the police wouldn't register a complaint until Tanya had been missing for at least twenty-four hours. I realized much later that she was trying to get me to delay calling the police for as long as possible,' she said.

By late evening on 21 September, as the police investigation was gathering steam, there was news from Nani Sankhyad village in Anklav, about 50 kilometres away. Local residents had seen the body of a young girl on the bank of the canal. They informed the local police, who strongly suspected at once that the body was that of seven-year-old Tanya.

Soon after she went missing, the Nadiad police had sent out an alert, which included a photograph of Tanya, to all police stations in the area. The police in Anklav reported that the body seemed to be hers but they couldn't be 100 per cent sure. In just five days, Tanya's body had decomposed severely and maggots crawled all over her body.

The Nadiad police prepared to send a team to Nani Sankhyad village on 21 September, and informed Tanya's relatives that one of them would have to come with them to identify her body. Filled with trepidation, Devyani, Tanya's aunt, stepped up to the difficult task.

On the journey to Nani Sankhyad, Devyani was prepared for the worst. But what she witnessed left her 'horrified and speechless'. The body she saw was not only bloated and decomposing, but was missing portions of all four limbs. The arms ended above the elbows and the legs between the ankles and knees.

Devyani said that Tanya's face was completely unrecognizable and that she only knew it was her because she recognized her clothes—grey, knee-length pants and a pink T-shirt. This, however, did not prove Tanya's identity beyond doubt. The police decided to wait for the post-mortem report for final confirmation.

The post-mortem, conducted at Shree Krishna hospital at Karamsad on 22 September, confirmed that the body was indeed Tanya's. The report noted blunt wounds to the back of her head and said the cause of death was 'haemorrhage inside the skull'. It did not, however, specify how Tanya may have suffered these injuries: Were they from the impact of the water 80 feet below the bridge, or did Meet kill her before throwing her off it? The police didn't seem to be entirely sure either.

The report noted that many of the injuries to Tanya's body occurred after her death and were the result—directly or indirectly—of being in water for a long time. Her body was found with her right eye and most of her hair missing. But perhaps the most gruesome part of the report concerned Tanya's hands and legs, which had 'gnawing injuries'. Rathod said, 'Her body travelled a long distance and passed through forest areas, where wolves or wild dogs may have chewed off her limbs.'

Once Tanya's body had been found, Meet was arrested and Vijay and Kunal placed in the custody of a juvenile home at Mehsana. By then, Meet had told the police all the details of his plan and the way in which he executed it. 'He told us that he didn't want to kill the girl but had no other choice. He knew that Tanya would reveal his identity if left alive. So he had intended to kill her right from the start, and taking the stone along in the car was preparation for that,' said Dhirubhai. He added that such a case of kidnapping and brutal murder had occurred for the first time in Nadiad in more than two decades.

After Meet was remanded in police custody, the involvement of his mother, Jigisha, and younger brother, Dhruv, in the crime came to light. It was Jigisha who had escorted Tanya to the car, while Dhruv had bought sleeping pills to subdue the girl in case she struggled or screamed. They were never used. The police visited their home to arrest them but found that the two had fled upon hearing about Meet's arrest. They were eventually arrested from Ambaji on 28 September.

The police investigation soon revealed what had propelled Meet to act so drastically. He, they found, had something of a gambling addiction: his habit of betting on cricket matches had put him Rs 10 lakh in debt. According to Rathod, Meet said during his interrogation that he had borrowed around Rs 6 lakh from Pinal Jain, a friend, to pay off part of his debt, but desperately needed more. He told the police that his debts were not just from gambling. He had recently borrowed money for medical expenses when his grandfather was admitted to a hospital, and had sold his television to repay some amount of the loan.

The police also recorded the statement of Meet's father, Vimal Kumar Vinubhai Patel, and determined that Meet, Jigisha and Dhruv had not included him in the plan. 'Meet's father did not have any role in the case. In his statement, he said that he was an alcoholic and as soon as he entered the house, his family would stop talking. They would simply give him a bottle of alcohol to keep him occupied,' said Dhirubhai. Following the incident, Vimal moved out of the house, and it has been lying vacant ever since.

Though no one had seen Meet kidnapping Tanya or throwing her off the bridge, the police had two crucial witnesses against the five people accused of committing the crime. The first was Anju, a neighbour, who said she briefly saw Meet sitting in a car near the gate, before she went indoors to get a candle for Jigisha, on the night Tanya vanished. The second was the shopkeeper of a Havmor ice-cream outlet, who said he remembered Meet buying Tanya an ice cream. The police said that he was possibly the last person who saw Tanya alive.

After recording his statement, the police began to scour the CCTV video footage from the Vasad toll plaza and soon came upon a white Hyundai i10 driven by a man who fit Meet's description. The car arrived at the toll plaza at 8.29 p.m., heading towards Vasad bridge, and returned at 8.45 p.m. The footage is the most important piece of electronic evidence, and the police sent it for forensic analysis at once.

* * *

As two of their suspects were juveniles, the police filed two charge sheets—one for Meet, Jigisha and Dhruv, and another for seventeen-year-old Vijay and sixteen-year-old Kunal—on 16 December 2017. Meet, Jigisha and Dhruv were charged with kidnapping, murder and criminal conspiracy under the IPC.

Apart from Kunal, whose family managed to hire a lawyer from Ahmedabad High Court, none of the suspects has yet found a lawyer willing to represent them. They are in Bilodara jail in Kheda district and haven't been granted bail despite submitting several pleas. The trial is yet to begin at the time of publishing.

In January 2018, the prosecution filed a plea in a juvenile justice court, asking that Vijay and Kunal be tried as adults owing to the heinous nature of the crimes. The advocate representing the prosecution, Sangharsh Bajpai, said that a psychological report, prepared after a government-approved psychologist spent several hours with the juveniles, indicated that, though minors, both were 'mentally capable' of committing the offences they had been charged with.[7] Bajpai fought hard to ensure that Vijay and even Kunal, who wasn't with Meet and Vijay when they kidnapped and murdered Tanya, be tried as adults.

Kunal's lawyer told the court that Meet had threatened the boy with dire consequences if he refused to participate in the crime or told anyone about Tanya's death. According to Bajpai, 'His lawyer argued that Meet had threatened to kill him if he told anyone about Tanya's death and that since Kunal had committed the crime out of fear, he could not be tried as an adult. My point was that if he was scared, he could have stayed back in Baroda and called his parents to tell them what had happened. But he did no such thing,' said Bajpai. He added that Tanya's body may have taken much longer to find had the kidnappers gone through with their plan to weigh her body down with a rock.

On 2 April 2018, the magistrate ruled in favour of the prosecution: Vijay and Kunal would be tried as adults. The case was transferred to the children's court,[8] where the trial

---

[7] From an interview with Sangharsh Bajpai in Nadiad on 25 January 2018.

[8] The JJ Act, 2015, defines 'Children's Court' as 'a court established under the Commission for Protection of Child Rights Act, 2005, or a Special Court under the Protection of Children from Sexual

will run parallel to that of Meet, Jigisha and Dhruv in the sessions court.

* * *

It has been the most difficult time for Kusumben, because in the past four years, her life had revolved around Tanya alone. A sprightly young girl, Tanya enjoyed learning new things at school and found mathematics more interesting than other subjects. 'She had once asked me to buy her a blackboard so that she could pretend to be a teacher and write on the blackboard while teaching herself,' said Kusumben. She loved going out with her grandmother and would often wear a pink dress on such occasions.

The tragic loss of the seven-year-old girl has been the toughest on her parents, who were unable to attend her last rites, which had to be done the same day as the body was found in a decomposed state. Amit and Gayatri, who have two other children including a three-year-old daughter and a year-old son, work in a store in Southall in the UK and weren't able to come to Nadiad due to visa-related complications.

The parents had no option but to watch the final rites of their child on videos posted on news websites. Just a few

---

Offences Act, 2012, wherever existing and where such courts have not been designated, the Court of Sessions having jurisdiction to try offences under the Act'. Section 18 of the Juvenile Justice Act says, 'Where the Board after preliminary assessment under Section 15 pass an order that there is a need for trial of the said child as an adult, then the Board may order transfer of the trial of the case to the Children's Court having jurisdiction to try such offences.'

months before the incident, they had intended to fly Tanya as well as Kusumben to the UK, but weren't able to acquire visas for them.

For Tanya's grandparents, the initial anger has given way to bitterness and grief. Kusumben says she is determined to see that justice is attained and hopes that the court sentences the suspects to death. She refers to Jigisha as 'the devil incarnate' and says she is yet to fathom how her next-door neighbours, who had attended Tanya's birthday party, could have kidnapped and murdered the child. Bhaubhai, simmering with rage, said the actions of Meet and his family had also tarnished the name of the Patel community.

Things have been particularly difficult for the families of the accused, especially the juveniles. While Vijay's parents are daily-wage labourers, Kunal's family is from a primarily agricultural background. Kunal's mother, Hemali,[9] however, hopes the judicial system will give her son a chance to mend his ways.[10] But her journey has been particularly harrowing as she struggles to wrap her head around the technicalities of the law.

While his mother was running from pillar to post to find a good defence lawyer, Kunal tried to kill himself in the observation home at Mehsana. In a letter to the Juvenile Justice Board, the superintendent of the observation home wrote that he tried to hang himself using a bed sheet.

But in the face of circumstances that would make an ordinary person wilt, Hemali has shown extraordinary grit. In the run-up to the trial, she has been doing everything she can

---

[9] Name changed as she is the mother of a juvenile accused.
[10] From an interview with Hemali in Nadiad on 25 January 2018.

to ensure that, if found guilty, he gets a shorter sentence than Meet and Vijay as he 'had nothing to do with the kidnapping or killing of Tanya'. 'He did nothing that brought harm to the girl,' she insists, adding that he only agreed to make the ransom call because Meet threatened to hurt him.

When she visits her son at the observation home, she sees a growing fear, anxiety and frustration in him. 'He is battling anxiety and depression. He can't understand why he can't come home even though he didn't do anything to harm the girl and told the police the truth,' she said. The most difficult part of every visit, she added, is not having any answers for him.

She added that the police treated her son badly. 'When they took him to the chowki for interrogation, they didn't think of contacting us. It was only when they produced him in court that my elder son found out about it and rushed to meet Kunal,' she said.

She alleged that the police handcuffed Kunal and beat him for two days. 'When the police picked him up, they said it was for riding a motorcycle without a licence, which is unfair. No policemen called to tell us that our son is in their custody despite knowing that he is a minor. No journalist ever came to ask us our side of the story,' she said.

Kunal, she said, was not a good student. He didn't have much interest in studies and had failed his class X board exams in 2016. 'He was interested in fixing motorbikes. He would often work on his own bike at home and hoped to one day set up a business. We wanted him to finish his studies first. He was supposed to retake the math and English exams he had failed in a few months,' she said. Vouching for his good character, Hemali said that he would often help her run the family business of growing cash crops like wheat and millet.

She insisted her son was a good person. She pointed to the social investigation report, which notes that Kunal 'bears good conduct in the society and his neighbours and school teachers did not have any complaint with him'. Arguing that her son didn't have 'a criminal mind or intention', she said that his role was limited to making the ransom call, an offence that did not fit the category of 'heinous crimes' as per Section 15 of the new Juvenile Justice Act.

She said, 'It is wrong to charge my son with kidnapping. He was naive and made the mistake of not telling anyone what he knew. But he didn't make the ransom call, and he definitely had nothing to do with the kidnapping or murder of the child. I don't know why he did it—out of fear, loyalty or greed—but if he is given a harsh sentence at this age, it will be a stigma on him for the rest of his life.'

Though she conceded that her son had made a mistake, she hoped that the court would consider his 'minimal role' in the crime and give him a second chance with a light sentence. Fortunately for her, Kunal was granted bail in May 2018. Though she is elated to have her son back home, she will now have to wait until the case reaches its legal conclusion.

* * *

I recall thinking that it would be a challenge to speak to Tanya's family members considering how traumatic it must have been for them to see the body before they disposed of her mortal remains. Despite several attempts, I was unable to get in touch with them before I arrived at Nadiad, and that worried me.

I was doubtful whether Kusumben would agree to speak with me at all, especially since she had maintained her distance from other journalists before. Without her, the story wouldn't be complete. With the help of a local journalist, I went to her society, hoping to find her at home. The house, however, was locked.

But luck eventually favoured me and I ran into her and Tanya's maternal grandfather, Bhaubhai, at the sessions court complex in Kheda. They were hesitant at first. They weren't fluent in Hindi so our conversation started on a shaky note. But as time passed, Kusumben felt comfortable sharing the details. Then, she as well as Bhaubhai held nothing back. A conversation that I had hoped would last at least fifteen to twenty minutes went on for a couple of hours, with us seated on rickety chairs in the sessions court complex.

Later, I visited Kusumben at her house. After two interactions with her, it became quite clear that she had never imagined her life without Tanya even though her daughter had left her in her care only for a short period of time. Suddenly, her purpose in life had disappeared, leaving her with nothing but the pain she still feels when she looks at Tanya's paintings and belongings from time to time.

Even though Tanya's grandparents have never dealt with the judiciary before, her paternal grandmother, Kusumben, and her maternal grandfather, Bhaubhai, have helped each other find the courage to keep the case going. It is admirable to watch them as they work together to get through the legal paperwork. In the absence of Tanya's parents, Bhaubhai and Kusumben feel that the responsibility lies with them to do everything that is necessary to ensure that all the accused be punished severely.

4

Utkarsh Verma, New Delhi

The memory of her thirteen-year-old brother, Utkarsh Verma, looking entranced at his five-month-old nephew is one his elder sister, Kanika Verma, remembers often. Ever since Nabhya was born, Kanika had always hoped that her youngest brother would be the close confidant and guide to her son that she had been for him.[1]

When they were kids, Kanika often babysat her funny and creative brother whenever their parents were out. Kanika, who is twelve years older than Utkarsh, reminisced about the day he wanted to ride his bicycle but realized that one of the tyres was deflated. He was about eight years old at the time. She volunteered to get the tyre fixed at a shop, but he respectfully refused because he didn't want to bother his sister. 'When I went to check on him, he was still trying to fix his bicycle. But I noticed an overpowering smell of perfume and I asked him about it. He gave me the most earnest look and said that

---

[1] From an interview with Kanika Verma in New Delhi on 30 May 2018.

71

he had used up an entire bottle of perfume trying to fill what he thought was air from the bottle into the tyre,' said Kanika, recalling the incident fondly.

Kanika moved to Ohio with her husband, Siddhartha Singh, in 2012. She visited her family with her five-month-old son after a year and a half, her second trip to India since she moved. Ever since Utkarsh had learnt of the newest member of the family, he was excited to meet him. Utkarsh also has a brother, Rishabh, who is ten years older than him.

Utkarsh's family hails from Jaswantpur in Uttar Pradesh and has owned a jewellery business for several generations. Around thirty years ago, his father, Mukesh, decided to take the business forward and moved to a locality called Raghubarpura in New Delhi. 'My father had a shop in the village but it was a small one. I wanted to make something of our own, so after I got married, I shifted to Delhi and set up a shop,' said Mukesh.

After spending three decades in Raghubarpura, Mukesh decided to shift his house and shop to another less congested locality of East Delhi called Rajgarh Colony in an area called Shahdara.

The search for a reliable builder led Mukesh to Anil Kumar Thakur, a neighbour whom his family knew well. When he approached Anil, he agreed to take up the contract of constructing Mukesh's house and shop at Rajgarh Colony.

After a significant portion of the house was completed, Mukesh and his family moved into their new home at Rajgarh Colony in October 2013, and the shop remained at Raghubarpura, about a kilometre away, while work on the new one continued. During this time, Anil's son, twenty-two-year-old Pratap Singh Sisodiya, who was helping his father out, would bring the material over and gradually became a regular visitor at the Vermas'. Here he met Mukesh's youngest son, Utkarsh, frequently. An affable child, Utkarsh was friendly with Pratap and would refer to him as *bhaiya*.

* * *

Accompanied by her husband, Siddhartha Singh, and her son, Kanika reached her parents' house in Rajgarh Colony at 1 a.m. on 17 November 2014. It was an emotional reunion, and everyone in her family was awake to receive them, barring Utkarsh, who had slept early since he had school the next day.

Utkarsh, however, was an early riser and was up by 5 a.m. After getting ready for school, he had a few minutes before the school van picked him up at 6 a.m. from a spot about 100 metres away from his house.

He seized the opportunity and went to his sister's room to spend some time with her and his nephew. Since Nabhya was asleep at the time, Utkarsh watched him quietly for a few minutes and before he left, turned to his sister and made her promise that she wouldn't step out of the house without him.

A doting sister, Kanika promised to wait for him to return. 'I only got to see him for a few minutes. But he promised to spend time with me and play with my son once he finished his tuition lessons in the evening after school,' she said.

Utkarsh was a student of Vivekananda School in Anand Vihar. A private school van rented by a few parents, which would ferry around fifteen to twenty students, picked him up from Satsang Marg every day around 6 a.m. Like every other weekday, on 18 November, Utkarsh went to school and around 2 p.m., was dropped off at the same location.

But unlike any other weekday, Utkarsh didn't come back home.

* * *

Back in the Verma household, everyone in the family was excited about meeting Nabhya. Mukesh left for his shop around 8 a.m., and his wife, Mamta, went about her usual chores.[2] Since her daughter was around, time flew by. In the afternoon, she realized that Utkarsh was running late.

It wasn't unusual for the school van to run behind its usual schedule due to heavy traffic, and on such days, Mamta would call the driver, Gurmeet Singh, to inquire about the delay. That day, when Utkarsh didn't return home by 2.25 p.m., Mamta called Gurmeet, expecting to hear about another traffic congestion. But she was perturbed when he told her that he had dropped Utkarsh off ten minutes ago.

Utkarsh usually came straight home. Anxious about her son's whereabouts, she immediately called her husband to check if Utkarsh had gone to meet him at the shop. It was not uncommon for him to visit his father after school.

But her heart sank when her husband told her otherwise. She started to panic. 'In the past, he has come to drop off my lunch on days I wasn't able to come home for lunch. But he would always go home first, drop off his bag, change

---

[2] From an interview with Mukesh Verma in New Delhi on 4 February 2018.

his clothes and then come to the shop. He would give me the lunch box and then run off for his tuition classes,' said Mukesh. Utkarsh would usually go for his tuition classes at 4 p.m., which would last an hour and a half.

At the same time, Kanika had stepped out of the house to make some purchases from the market nearby for her cousin's upcoming wedding, and she had taken her mother's phone. She received a call from her mother, who asked for the phone numbers of Utkarsh's classmates saved on her phone. Mamta hoped that perhaps Utkarsh may have gone with his friends and would come back home soon. As soon as she heard her mother's troubled voice, Kanika immediately sensed something was wrong and rushed back home.

Meanwhile, Mukesh tried to think of places his son may have gone off to. He figured that his wife may have misheard the cab driver. He called up Gurmeet to double-check, only to get the same response his wife got. Mukesh's next call was to his nephew, Rajat Verma, who had a shop called Sree Jewellers on Chand Mohalla just 50 metres away from the spot where Utkarsh's van dropped him. Rajat, however, told him that he hadn't seen Utkarsh that day.

Mukesh tried to maintain his composure. Along with his elder son, Rishabh, he set out on a scooter to look for Utkarsh in the busy market area around their house, hoping to find him eating at a stall nearby. But in his heart, Mukesh knew that Utkarsh would never go anywhere without informing someone in the family.

As the word spread, Mukesh's neighbours came out to help him look for his son in the park and other nearby areas. After an unsuccessful search, at 3.45 p.m., Mukesh decided that it

was time to seek help from the police. He went to Gandhi
Nagar police station where he met the station house officer,
Manoj Pant. The police collected the relevant information
and by 4.30 p.m., a case of kidnapping was registered.

When Mukesh filed the complaint with the police, he
was certain that someone had lured Utkarsh away, since he
would never go anywhere with a stranger. He gave them
the photograph he found in Utkarsh's old report card, and
the police immediately posted the picture on group chats on
WhatsApp. Manoj, simultaneously, informed all the police
control room (PCR) vans in the neighbourhood to keep an
eye out for the boy.[3]

Sanjay Beniwal, the then joint commissioner of the
Eastern Range, remembered the case to be a challenging
one due to the lack of clues.[4] He added that the teams of
policemen had an arduous task ahead of questioning all those
who were regular visitors or close to the family. 'I remember
the emotional imprint and the trouble of the boy's parents.
They were well off, so it was a humongous task. Everyone from
the plumber to the neighbours, relatives and distant relatives
(whoever had come to their house) had to be meticulously
ruled out,' he said.

Mukesh, along with the police, reached his house at
around 6 p.m. and started looking for CCTV cameras in the
area. A team of around twenty to twenty-five police officials
led by Inspector Krishan Gopal Tyagi were assigned to

---

[3]   From an interview with Manoj Pant in New Delhi on 3 February
      2018.
[4]   From an interview with Sanjay Beniwal in New Delhi on 2
      February 2018.

the case, and together, they started questioning the family members for more details.[5]

Shortly after, they were able to procure the footage from the camera of the J.D.M. Public School nearby, which showed Utkarsh walking towards home at 2.15 p.m. The police noticed that there was one lane in the middle near Babbar Jewellers which wasn't entirely visible in the footage from the closest CCTV camera. The police were confident that whatever had happened after Utkarsh was dropped off had taken place in that lane, as it was the only route Utkarsh could have taken.

The search for clues from other CCTV cameras resulted in an inordinate amount of footage. Precious time was running out, and the police had to scan through all of it. Beniwal said that they had to scan around ten hours of video footage.

Word about the case spread quickly. The police soon had endless queries from the media to deal with. 'The pressure from the media was unrelenting. It was close to election time, and the case was beginning to pick up political overtones. Everyone was making comments on it. Not that anyone was hounding us but then one gets psyched in such a situation,' said a senior police official on condition of anonymity.

While the various teams of policemen were busy looking for constructive leads, Mamta's mobile phone rang at 7.22 p.m.

Mamta was at home when she received the call while her husband was downstairs with the police. The caller said, '*Tera launda mere paas hai. Ek crore ka intezam kar le* (Your son is with me. You have to arrange for Rs 1 crore).'

---

[5] From an interview with Krishan Gopal Tyagi in New Delhi on 3 February 2018.

Mamta, who is otherwise a mild-mannered woman, couldn't control herself. Kanika, who was sitting with her mother, said that right after she answered the call, she started shouting into the phone and kept saying, 'Where is my son? Send him home right now,' until the kidnapper disconnected the call.

Mukesh and the police officials rushed upstairs as soon as they heard Mamta's screams. After relaying the short conversation with the kidnapper, she mentioned an odd detail. 'My wife said that the caller had a weird voice that sounded like a woman's. We later realized that the kidnapper had used a mobile application to mask his actual voice,' said Mukesh.

The police immediately noted the number and tried to trace it, only to find that it had been purchased on a fake identity document as the details on the ID didn't check out. While Mukesh and his family members were waiting for an update, at 8.43 p.m., the kidnapper made a second call using a different SIM card, this time on Mukesh's mobile number. But Mukesh was ready and he recorded the conversation on his phone.

In the second call, the kidnapper didn't disguise his voice and said, 'Sit quietly wherever you are. There is no need to tell anyone around you. I want money. I will tell you in the morning where to bring the money.' At this point, Mukesh asked him who he was and where he was calling from. The kidnapper reacted in anger and disconnected the call, repeating that he would call the next morning with further directions.

Terrified, Mukesh tried to call back on the number but found it to be switched off. He immediately went to the police station to inform them about the phone call.

Expectedly, the second number too had been purchased on a fake identity card.

Despite listening to the recording of the phone conversation several times, Mukesh was unable to recognize the voice. The police analysed the call data records of all the people whom Mukesh suspected. The police also started tracing the calls made to Mukesh's mobile number since they expected the kidnappers to call again on 19 November. They advised him to prolong the conversation as much as possible.

Exhausted, Mukesh returned home at 1 a.m. 'I didn't try to arrange for the money, since we all thought that the kidnapper would negotiate on the ransom amount. I had hoped that when the kidnapper called in the morning, the police would be able to trace his call, find my son and bring him back home safely,' said Mukesh.

Sleep was out of the question, and everyone in the family, including relatives who had come to offer moral support, spent the next few hours doing the only thing that they could— wait. At 6 a.m., Mukesh had a bath and waited for the call he was almost certain he would receive. What happened next, however, made absolutely no sense to him or the policemen who had spent the entire night trying to find the boy.

After working the entire night, Manoj went back home to have a quick shower before he got back into the search for Utkarsh. At 7.15 a.m., he received a call from one of the officers who told him that a body of a boy dressed in school uniform had been found in a drain near the Ramlila Maidan. 'I was at home when I got the news, and I realized that the worst possible outcome had happened. I bolted out of my house and rushed to the spot. When I got there, there was just a PCR van parked nearby,' said Manoj.

Mukesh was waiting patiently by his phone when he received a call from a police official around 8 a.m. saying that they had found a body. He was numb when he was asked to come and identify the body.

As the last rays of hope deserted him, Mukesh steeled himself. Accompanied by his son, he went to the location, which was just 200 metres away from his house.

Mukesh found his son's body in a shallow drain filled with water with his face shoved into the mud and his leg sticking out of the drain. Utkarsh was still dressed in his school uniform—a white shirt, a pair of black trousers and a tie.

The report was filed under a case of unnatural death caused by violence and mentioned that the body had certain injuries, including bite marks over the left forearm and signs of injury on the left foot as well as on the neck, among others. The post-mortem of his body was conducted at the Aruna Asaf Ali Government Hospital in Civil Lines, and the report identified the cause of death to be asphyxiation as a result of throttling and smothering.

Now that the body had been found, ensuring the safety of the child was no longer the police's priority. All this time, they had tried to keep away from Utkarsh's house to avoid alerting the kidnappers who may be monitoring the house from a distance. But once the body was recovered, they had to change their strategy.

The police knew that Utkarsh had disappeared just 150 metres away from his house and that he wouldn't leave with a stranger. 'It was a busy market. If someone forcibly tried to take him, Utkarsh would have made some noise and attracted the attention of people passing by. The kidnapper would have to be someone known to him,' said Krishan. But the list of people Utkarsh was likely to go along with was surprisingly short and included his brother and a domestic help.

The police had to consider all options. This included organized gangs, former kidnappers and local goons, who were eventually ruled out. After call data records of the neighbours, relatives and other frequent visitors did not yield any new leads, Krishan asked Mukesh once again for the names of people who knew Utkarsh well. This time the list included twenty-two-year-old Pratap, his builder Anil's son.

The police started checking the call data records of all these people for any anomalies. Pratap's records threw up something strange. He had made calls to a particular number an unusually large number of times.

Following the clue, Krishan decided to check out the call records of that number, which belonged to twenty-two-year-old Siddharth, Pratap's friend. The call records revealed a curious coincidence. 'We had traced the location of the number from which the second ransom call was made. While analysing Siddharth's data, we found that at 8.43 p.m., his tower location matched the location of the caller who had made the ransom call,' he said.

When the police continued to look at his call records, Krishan noticed that compared to the call records on other days, on 18 November, there was an abnormal number of calls received and made from Siddharth's phone.

They continued to dig further. While Pratap's phone was switched off for most of the day, the police found that the tower location of Siddharth's phone placed him at the spot where the body was found as well.

News reports mentioned that a week after the body was found, the police interrogated more than 400 people and

finally zeroed in on Pratap and Siddharth.[6] Krishan said
that they had issued a notice under Section 160 of the Code
of Criminal Procedure Act (CrPC)[7] to several people who
may have had relevant information pertaining to the case,
including Pratap and Siddharth, both of whom showed up at
the police station.

The special public prosecutor, Bhupinder Singh Joon, said
that the duo was arrested on 25 November after Siddharth
mentioned Pratap's name in his confession.[8] The police
claimed that after the interrogation, neither of them were
able to deny their role in the crime and confessed to killing
the boy. Joint Commissioner Sanjay recalled that when the
two men were arrested, both insisted that they were innocent.
But after prolonged questioning, the police claimed that their
stories fell apart.

Elaborating on the techniques used during interrogation,
Sanjay said that the police often asked questions about the
sequence of events in the reverse order to determine if a person
was guilty. Stories unravel in the process and are among the
telltale signs that give them away.

---

6 https://timesofindia.indiatimes.com/city/delhi/Failed-actor-
   arrested-for-kidnap-murder-of-Utkarsh/articleshow/45278673.cms
7 Section 160 of the CrPC Act states: Any police officer, making
   an investigation under this Chapter may, by order in writing,
   require the attendance before himself of any person being within
   the limits of his own or any adjoining station who, from the
   information given or otherwise, appears to be acquainted with the
   facts and circumstances of the case; and such person shall attend
   as so required. See https://www.oecd.org/site/adboecdanti-
   corruptioninitiative/46814340.pdf
8 From an interview with Bhupinder Singh Joon in New Delhi on
   7 February 2018.

On 18 November, just before Utkarsh's van reached its scheduled stop, Pratap hid in a narrow lane nearby on a black Honda Activa scooter which belonged to Siddharth. When the van dropped Utkarsh off, Pratap called out to him.

He allegedly told Utkarsh that his grandmother had passed away and his parents weren't at home. 'Pratap convinced the boy that his father had asked him to pick him up and take him to where Mukesh and his family were. Since Utkarsh knew him well, he got on the motorbike and went along with him,' said Inspector Krishan.

Closely trailing behind him was Siddharth, riding Pratap's Royal Enfield Bullet. Krishan believed that the duo thought of swapping their motorbikes since they felt a Bullet would attract more attention in a bustling market area than a common scooter. They did not want to risk being noticed with the boy and increase their chances of being caught.

They had planned the kidnapping down to the last detail. They would sedate Utkarsh to prevent him from making a noise or trying to escape. Before meeting him at the stop, Siddharth had allegedly purchased a strip of tablets, a mild tranquillizer, and mixed a few of them in a bottle of water.

Pratap first took Utkarsh to a shop selling fruit juice. But before he handed him the glass of juice, he offered him the bottle of water and urged him to have a few sips.

Utkarsh obliged. In a matter of few minutes, he began to feel drowsy. By then, Pratap had taken him up to the third floor to his two-bedroom apartment in East Guru Angad Nagar where he lived with his fiancée, Urvashi Sakhare. Pratap took a semi-conscious Utkarsh to the bedroom.

The two had their own roles to play. While Pratap stayed at home to keep a watch over Utkarsh, it was Siddharth's responsibility to make the ransom calls and monitor the movements of the police at Utkarsh's house. After making the first ransom call on Mamta's phone, Siddharth kept watch on the Verma household for any changes.

The news about the kidnapping of a young child had already spread in the neighbourhood, and people had started to gather in front of their gate. 'After making the second ransom call, Siddharth waited near our house for more than an hour. When he saw a lot of people, he realized that the police were here and he called Pratap to tell him that things were not looking good,' said Mukesh.

Neither Pratap nor Siddharth were hardened criminals. They were both edgy amateurs. A passing PCR van doing its usual rounds was enough to spark off panic in Pratap's mind. 'It is normal for PCR vans to take rounds of an area at night. But since they were already nervous about getting caught, they thought that the police had found out about them and any moment they would come knocking at their door,' said Manoj.

By the time Siddharth went back to the flat, the effect of the sedatives they had given to Utkarsh had completely worn off. Both of them knew they had little time before Utkarsh would start crying for help, which could attract the attention of the neighbours or another passing PCR van. The duo then realized that killing Utkarsh was the only option left.

Inspector Krishan said that Pratap first sat on him, placed a pillow over his face and tried to suffocate him. Possibly due to an adrenaline rush, Utkarsh put up a tough fight and they were unable to kill him.

Unsuccessful, they allegedly took turns to stand on his neck while the other held his arms.

Even though Sanjay has dealt with many kidnapping cases in his career, this one affected him emotionally. 'We were so depressed to see the body, especially since we had tried so hard to rescue him. I think they became insane after a point. They didn't even know how to strangle someone. How can a human being do something like this?' he said.

After killing Utkarsh, Pratap and Siddharth had to figure out a way to dispose of the body. At around 5 a.m. on 19 November, when Mukesh was at home expecting the third call from the kidnappers, the two of them left Pratap's house with Utkarsh's body.

While Pratap rode the motorbike, Siddharth sat behind him with Utkarsh's body in the middle. When they reached Ramlila Maidan, they threw the body into the drain. Much later, Mukesh came to know that they had shoved Utkarsh's face into the muddy water in the drain to ensure that he wasn't alive.

* * *

Apart from the electronic evidence, the police have an important witness against the two accused—Pratap's fiancée, Urvashi, who was also in the apartment that day. She had been locked in one of the two bedrooms of the house but had heard everything that had happened that day.

During his interrogation, Pratap mentioned that Urvashi was in the flat on the day of the incident. Urvashi was there when the police reached Pratap's house. Inspector Krishan said that the police first ascertained her knowledge about the boy and ensured that she had no direct role in the crime before making her a witness in the case.

According to her written statement she had given in the presence of a magistrate, Urvashi, a resident of Nagpur, claimed that she was engaged to Pratap and had come to New Delhi to prepare for the civil services examinations. About a week before Pratap was arrested, she stated that he had told her that he was facing some financial problems in his business. A day later, he mentioned his intention of kidnapping a child, something she dismissed as a joke at the time.

On 18 November, she was at home, when around 3 p.m., Pratap and Siddharth entered the house with a boy dressed in his school uniform. When she inquired about the boy, Pratap told her that he had kidnapped him, as he had said he would.

She was taken aback by his response and asked him to return the boy to his family. Pratap then told her that he had kidnapped the boy for a noted gangster known as Asif Bhai who was on his way to the flat to collect the boy. He also threatened her with dire consequences if she mentioned this to anyone.

Scared out of her wits, she left the flat and went to Pratap's father Anil's house in Geeta Colony. Later that evening, when she returned to the flat, Siddharth and Pratap were still there with the boy.

When she entered her bedroom, Pratap asked her to get some sleep and locked the door from the outside. She claimed that at the time, she wasn't able to contact anyone to ask for help since her phone battery had died and Pratap had taken her charger away. Around 10.30 p.m., she heard the boy's voice demanding that he be allowed to speak to his parents over the phone. Utkarsh was fed sedatives once again and silenced.

In hindsight, both the police and Mukesh unanimously feel that the kidnappers did not have any plan to let Utkarsh go back home alive. 'If Pratap had allowed Utkarsh to go home, he would have surely revealed his identity. If he didn't release him, then the police would have eventually caught him. So either way, they knew they had to kill him even after taking the money,' said Mukesh.

* * *

The police claimed that Pratap and Siddharth had purchased five SIM cards and five cheap handsets to make the ransom calls using fake identity cards. Apart from confiscating their personal phones, the police also recovered two SIM cards and handsets. One was found outside the V3S Mall in Shahdara, while the other one was picked up by a passer-by who later produced the phone at the police station. They were unable to find the other three.

A day after their arrest, the details given by Pratap and Siddharth led the police to the rented flat in East Guru Angad Nagar. There they found the bill for the pills they had used to sedate Utkarsh and the receipt for the purchase of the two mobile phones that were used for making the ransom calls.

They found Utkarsh's belongings, including his gold locket which had the image of a Hindu goddess, Sherawali Mata, tied to a black string, his watch and his school identity card at the flat. The police also came across Pratap's shoes. They analysed the sample of mud taken from the sole and found that it matched the soil from the area where Utkarsh's body had been dumped.

Pratap and Siddharth led the police to a black polythene bag in the bushes near the Sub-divisional Magistrate (East) Office in Geeta Colony on 27 November which contained a school bag, a pair of black shoes and socks, all of which belonged to Utkarsh. Later that day, the police seized the Bullet belonging to Pratap, as well as Siddharth's black scooter.

Even though they both wanted a large sum of money in a short period of time, the police insisted that the plan was put together by Pratap.

Following their arrest, a news report stated that prior to the incident, Pratap had pursued a course in acting at the ICE (Institute of Creative Excellence) Institute in Mumbai.[9]

Mukesh added that during his stay in Mumbai, Pratap had tried to find modelling assignments for about eight months before calling it quits and moving back to New Delhi. 'While he was in Mumbai, his father sent him money every month. But after he noticed that his son was straying, he stopped giving him money, forcing Pratap to return back home,' said Mukesh.

When Pratap came to New Delhi, he brought his fiancée, Urvashi, along and rented the flat in East Guru Angad Nagar for both of them. However, since he was unemployed and his father had stopped sending money, he wasn't able to retain the lifestyle he had back in Mumbai. Hoping to start his own business, Pratap had opened a call centre in Noida with a friend but was unable to keep it running.

In the statement released after their arrest, the police claimed that during their interrogation, Pratap had disclosed

---

[9] https://timesofindia.indiatimes.com/city/delhi/Failed-actor-arrested-for-kidnap-murder-of-Utkarsh/articleshow/45278673.cms

that he needed Rs 20 lakh for the call centre. He came up with the plan of kidnapping a child for ransom and roped in his friend Siddharth as well.

The police claimed that Pratap had even carried out a mock drill of his plan on 14 November at the place where Utkarsh's school van dropped him off. He met Utkarsh that day and asked him about his school timings.

His accomplice, Siddharth, was a mobile repair technician, and like Pratap, he too wanted to set up a business of his own, dealing with car accessories. After completing class XII, Siddharth was not keen on joining college. 'He was weak in studies and didn't have much of an interest in attending regular college. He was open to pursuing a correspondence course. He started repairing mobile phones on the side since he wanted to help his mother financially,' said Neeru Sharma, his aunt.[10] She added that he eventually took up a six-month-long course in mobile repairing from a private institute and soon after started working at a friend's shop.

Pratap was desperate for the money. The police claimed that his first target was his eight-year-old cousin, Vibhu, whose father was a property dealer. He, however, changed his mind when he realized Utkarsh would make a far easier target, and he could extract a bigger ransom from Mukesh as he was a jeweller.

* * *

---

[10] From an interview with Neeru Sharma in New Delhi on 9 February 2018.

Even as he tried to make sense of the reason behind it all, Mukesh felt that Pratap was always confident that even if they got into trouble with the police, his father, who was a builder and had connections in the police department, would help them get away with it.

Apart from Urvashi, the police gathered other witnesses to build their case, including the juice vendor who allegedly saw Pratap with Utkarsh, and the employee of the pharmacy who sold the pills to Siddharth. Krishan added that they also found a CCTV camera installed in a house near Pratap's flat in East Guru Angad Nagar, which shows Pratap riding the scooter with Utkarsh seated behind him. Even though Special Public Prosecutor Bhupinder Singh Joon is confident that he has a strong case, he feels that the police made a big mistake in making Urvashi a witness instead of arresting her. He has moved an application at the Karkardooma court in New Delhi with a plea that Urvashi be summoned by the court as an accused and face charges, including causing disappearance of evidence or giving false information to screen offender, in this case, Pratap, her fiancé.

The application further added that Urvashi was legally bound to inform the police about the offence and alleged that she had intentionally remained quiet about it. If rumours were to be believed, an unnamed source stated that the police did not arrest her due to political pressure from a certain member of Parliament from Nagpur, the city she hails from.

While the application demanding that Urvashi be treated as an accused is yet to be taken up in court, Bhupinder has moved another application demanding interim compensation of Rs 10 lakh for the day-to-day maintenance of Mukesh's shop.

* * *

The case is currently pending at the Karkardooma court and is a long way from reaching its legal conclusion. But Mukesh has made it a point to attend every hearing despite knowing that he will have to face the people accused of killing his son. Since the incident, Anil and Mukesh haven't exchanged a single word. Like Mukesh, Anil comes for every hearing with his relatives in a show of support for Pratap.

Both the accused were initially kept at Tihar Jail, and during that time, Pratap contracted an infection in his lungs. In March 2017, he was diagnosed with pulmonary tuberculosis.

Pratap's advocate, Rajiv Mohan, applied for bail twice last year on medical grounds, and he was denied both times since the report filed by the jail authorities stated that his condition was stable and they are capable of managing the ailment.[11] While in judicial custody, he received treatment from numerous hospitals, including the All India Institute of Medical Sciences in New Delhi.[12]

However, a couple of days after Pratap was diagnosed, two of the inmates at Tihar Jail died of illness, after which a

---

[11] From an interview with Rajiv Mohan in New Delhi on 6 February 2018.

[12] According to the 'Medical Status Report of inmate patient Pratap Singh s/o Anil Kumar' issued by the Office of the Senior Medical Officer, Dispensary, Central Jail No. 03, Tihar, New Delhi, on 11 January 2018 (Document No. MO I.C./CJ-03/2018/0169-70).

medical board was constituted on 10 January. After assessing the condition of the inmates who were suffering from terminal illnesses, the board published a report the next day.

In this report, the jail authorities included Pratap's name in the list of seriously/terminally sick inmates and added that his treatment was not possible in jail.[13] 'The jail authorities recommended that if the court wants, bail can be granted to him after evaluating his illness. We then approached the Delhi High Court and he was granted bail on 2 February 2018 for a period of four months so that he can get further medical treatment,' said Rajiv. At the end of four months, the court granted him an extension till 25 July.

Rajiv said that due to the illness, Pratap had lost a lot of weight. The man, who is over six feet tall and weighed around 80 kilograms back in 2014, currently weighs only 49 kilograms. After he was diagnosed with tuberculosis, fluid started to build up in his lungs, and he had to be rushed to the hospital where they created a permanent passage to drain the fluid. Due to weakness in his limbs, he is brought in for the hearings in a wheelchair.

Despite all the evidence at hand, Rajiv feels that the police implicated the two men and they have no plausible explanation for committing such a grave crime, especially since Pratap belonged to a wealthy family. 'Pratap has had no criminal history and the police have a case built on

---

[13] According to the report titled 'Examination of Seriously Sick/ Terminally Ill Patients by Members of Committee at the office of Senior Medical Officer, Central Jail Hospital' signed by the Chairman of the Terminally Ill Patients Review Committee and four other members on 5 January 2018 (Document No. MO I.C./CJ-03/2018/0063-67).

circumstantial evidence which cannot prove [the charges] with certainty. Such evidence can be created as well,' said Rajiv. He argued that the police had framed him only on the basis of a suspicion that Pratap knew Utkarsh's father.

Opposing the police's version of events, Rajiv also alleged that they illegally detained Pratap and falsely implicated him in the case after torturing him. Rajiv claimed that the police had gone to Pratap's house at 3 a.m. on 25 November and asked him to accompany them as part of their investigation.

When asked where Pratap was on 18 November 2014, however, Rajiv replied that his family did not have a proper answer for it. He added that his job was to counter the points raised by the prosecution, and based on the charge sheet, it doesn't seem as though Pratap had any involvement.

His counterpart, Bhupinder, feels confident that both Pratap and Siddharth will be convicted for the brutal murder they allegedly committed. Considering the terminal nature of Pratap's illness, he said, 'If Pratap survives this disease, he will face conviction. If he dies, then only Siddharth will face the charges.'

Like the Vermas, the incident has left Siddharth's family deeply disturbed too. None of them could have imagined that he could do something like this to a small child, especially since he took such good care of his young cousins. Even though Siddharth's family found it difficult to accept the facts of the case, they blame Pratap for luring Siddharth into his plan. 'Siddharth only thought that he would help Pratap get Utkarsh and then get the money in the end. He didn't think he would have any further involvement and never imagined that things would end up like this,' said Siddharth's aunt, Neeru.

When she met him in jail after his arrest, she asked him whether he ever stopped to consider that the boy knew Pratap well and would surely have told his parents if he ever went home. But the only response she got was that at the time, money was the only thought on his mind.

While she didn't deny Siddharth's alleged role in Utkarsh's kidnapping, she believed that he had no role to play in the boy's murder. 'We have a lot of sympathy for Utkarsh's family. But Siddharth had no hand in the murder of the child. When Pratap asked him to help him strangle Utkarsh, he flatly refused,' she said.

Even though the trial has a long way to go, Siddharth's family members said that he seemed to have given up. 'He keeps saying that he will end up spending his entire life in jail and asks us why we keep coming to visit him. Sometimes he even says that he doesn't want a lawyer and that we should get rid of him and not waste money,' said Neeru.

While his family is still hoping for the best outcome, Neeru alleges that Pratap has been trying to pressurize Siddharth into taking the entire blame on himself. 'He tried to bribe him and promised him a flat for his mother. He almost succeeded in convincing Siddharth but we managed to talk him out of it,' she said.

While their fate is in the hands of the law, Utkarsh's family has tried to cope with the loss of the most loved member of the family in their own way. A framed photograph of Utkarsh sits on the desk of Mukesh's shop with fresh flowers around it. After he shifted his shop to Rajgarh Colony in 2015, Mukesh decided to change the name of his shop from Mukesh Jewellers to Utkarsh Jewellers, with the wish that his son's name lives on.

Utkarsh was a significant part of Kanika's life, and she knows that no matter how much time passes, she will always remember his antics and friendly nature. Though time has played a significant role in helping her deal with the loss, she misses the numerous conversations she would have daily with Utkarsh over video calls. Utkarsh's mother, Mamta, found it harder to cope with the sudden loss of her son and didn't speak to anyone for several months.

Even though Kanika was emotionally shaken, she couldn't think of leaving her mother alone and heading back home. A couple of months later, her brother Rishabh got married, and his wife was able to take care of Mamta, giving Kanika the confidence to move back to her life in the US.

But now and then, memories come rushing back, and they try their best to remember the good times. 'Last year when the board examination results came out, my mother and I spoke about how Utkarsh would have done so well. It has been a tough couple of years for me, but I have learnt to cherish whatever we have in our lives,' Kanika said.

Once in a while, Kanika's son, Nabhya, who is now four years old, asks about his Utkarsh mama (uncle) when he scrolls through family photographs. She is happy that she gets to relive the funny and happy memories she has of Utkarsh while recounting them to her child.

* * *

Even time, sometimes, cannot heal everything. In kidnapping cases, family members of victims who go through the trauma of losing a loved one are often reluctant to meet journalists to avoid revisiting the painful memories. Utkarsh's family stood out among others. They were kind, warm and welcoming. But speaking about their beloved son and brother wasn't an easy task for them, and they often choked while recounting their fond memories of him. But they unanimously felt that telling his story might help another family cope with their loss or help parents take precautions to ensure the safety of their children.

Despite the emotions that flooded his mind every time he saw Pratap and Siddharth being brought into the courtroom at Karkardooma Sessions Court, Mukesh, Utkarsh's father, attended every hearing and was well versed with the details of the case. On the day I went to meet him, he didn't need any documents to recollect the chronology of events more accurately than some of the lawyers I encountered.

Utkarsh's case is also among the few wherein I had the opportunity of interacting with the family of one of the accused, and it gave me a glimpse into their difficult predicament. Though suspicious at first, Siddharth's aunt and other members of his family eventually opened up about the tough spot he had put them in. Siddharth's long legal fight has now become theirs as well. The consequences of his alleged actions have impacted the lives of his entire family who now run to court every time there is a hearing and visit him in prison whenever they can.

5

Abhay Modani, Hyderabad

In a small, one-room apartment in Hindi Nagar, Hyderabad, in early 2016, three ambitious men in their early twenties huddled together to watch a Telugu thriller called *Oka Romantic Crime Katha* on a mobile phone. Two characters in the movie, a fifteen-year-old girl and her boyfriend, kidnap, rob and kill eight people to fulfil their dreams of an opulent life.

A film can affect different people differently. While for some it is simply entertainment, for others it can mean much more. Once in a while, films can inspire people to do things they are unlikely to consider otherwise. The popular 2012 Telugu film focused on issues such as teenage love, sex and abortions.[1]

The storyline of the movie revolves around three teenage girls falling for the wrong guys and how they end up committing irreversible mistakes. One of the girls, Tanmayi,

---

[1]   https://www.news18.com/news/india/orck-50-days-of-sucess-in-24-centers-494773.html

97

and her boyfriend, Sanjay, rob and then kill eight people just
to get rich.[2]

The plot appealed so much to twenty-year-old
Indugamalli Sheshu Kumar, twenty-one-year-old Pondara
Ravi and twenty-three-year-old Namburi Mohan that a
couple of months later they made up their minds to kidnap
a child for ransom. The three resorted to such an extreme
measure in the hope of fulfilling their dream of becoming
successful film actors, for which they required an exorbitant
sum of money.

* * *

Overambitious twenty-year-old Sheshu, whom his friends
called Sai, worked as a domestic help for an elderly man in
Sree Colony at Begum Bazaar. After watching the film, he
had a target in mind—Abhay Modani. Abhay and Abhishek
Modani were fourteen-year-old twins who lived next door to
where he worked.

Sheshu frequently met the twins, both class X students
of Slate School in Abids, in the evenings, when the children
in the neighbourhood got together to play cricket. He forged
a close friendship with Abhay over three months, and the
two often spent their free time watching videos on Abhay's
phone. They knew each other well enough for Abhay to lend
Sheshu his Honda Activa, which they often took for a spin
together.

---

[2] https://timesofindia.indiatimes.com/entertainment/
    telugu/movie-reviews/oka-romantic-crime-katha/movie-
    review/14155282.cms

Abhay's family owned a plastic recycling business, while Sheshu's upbringing was less privileged. He had moved to Hyderabad from Rajahmundry to work as a caretaker at Sri Karthikeya Foundation, an old-age home. It was through this organization that he came to work for the Daraks who lived next door to the Modanis. He took care of an elderly man at their house, earning Rs 6000 a month.

Soon, Sheshu, who lived in a one-room flat with Ravi, realized that Abhay was from a wealthy family. During their numerous casual conversations over copious glasses of tea or while having pani puri, Sheshu observed that Abhay used expensive mobile phones and often spoke about the comfortable life he led.

Ravi also worked for Sri Karthikeya Foundation and had been assigned to care for a senior citizen at Gachibowli. After the two moved in together, they reached out to Mohan in Srikakulum, who was unemployed at the time, and asked him to move in with them. The police investigation would later reveal that the three had known each other for two years, having met as workers at a steel factory in Ranchi.

The three had bonded over movies and shared a dream of becoming actors. After moving in together, they watched countless movies, re-enacted scenes and practised dance steps to hone their skills.

Determined to fulfil their ambition, the three searched the Internet for people in the Hindi film industry with whom they could get in touch. Their search led them to a film director, whom they claimed to have found through Facebook, and who quickly doused their filmy dreams with a bucket of cold reality. To land the role of a lead character in a film—any film—would cost them at least Rs 10 lakh, he said.

As they racked their brains for a way to come up with this mildly ridiculous sum of money, they would later tell the police, Sheshu's mind went back to the last movie they had watched together. Once they had settled on kidnapping someone, it didn't take long to choose a target—Abhay.

Next, they chalked out the plan's finer details. Sheshu would use his friendship with Abhay to their advantage. They picked a day they would execute the plan. The Modanis live in Begum Bazaar, the largest commercial market in the old part of Hyderabad city, and Sheshu and his friends knew they couldn't afford to draw too much attention to themselves. Considering the crowded streets, they planned their escape routes.

Taking their cue from movies where kidnappers commonly stick tape over the mouth of their captives, they bought duct tape from a shop in Begum Bazaar. They even took steps to ensure that no one would miss them once they had disappeared with Abhay.

On 9 March, days before they were to kidnap Abhay, Sheshu visited the Daraks and told them he would be going away to his village for a month or two, promising to find them a replacement. Next, he told his boss at the Sri Karthikeya Foundation about his planned absence.

Sheshu and his friends stayed indoors for the next few days, planning the kidnapping. They decided that Sheshu alone would bring Abhay to the room, while the other two would stay put to avoid attracting attention.

Around 4.30 p.m. on 16 March, Abhay set out from home on his Honda Activa to buy idlis from Mahalaxmi Tiffin Centre, about half a kilometre away. Sheshu, who knew Abhay's daily routine, waited in an adjacent lane to avoid being spotted by any of Abhay's family members or even the neighbours. Investigating officer Rama Krishna said Sheshu knew in advance which route Abhay would take.[3] 'They had become close and Abhay had told Sheshu about a girl he liked, who lived on the lane adjacent to his house. Sheshu knew that Abhay would often drive by her building to catch a glimpse of her,' he said.

Sheshu lay in wait for a while but then began to wonder if Abhay had decided not to buy idlis that day. Then he saw the Modanis' domestic help, G. Vaishnavi, walking by. Rama said, 'He stopped her and asked if she had seen Abhay. She told him he had gone to the hospital with his mother and would be back in some time.' After returning from the hospital, Abhay set out to buy idlis.

After picking up his parcel from the tiffin centre, on his way back, Abhay entered the main gate of the colony and then took a U-turn to ride past the girl's house.

Around 5 p.m., Sheshu finally saw Abhay on his blue Honda Activa, wearing a black T-shirt and black jeans.

Abhay soon noticed his friend and stopped the scooter. Sheshu asked him what he was up to and whether he could get a ride home. Abhay agreed at once.

Halfway through their journey, Sheshu asked Abhay if he could ride the scooter the rest of the way. Abhay was oblivious to Sheshu's intentions and agreed to ride pillion. Before they switched positions, Sheshu telephoned his friends in secret and gave them an update.

Once they reached Hindi Nagar, Sheshu parked the scooter and telephoned his friends one last time as a heads-up

---

[3]   From an interview with Rama Krishna in Hyderabad on 9 December 2017.

before inviting Abhay upstairs. Abhay took the scooter key from Sheshu, stored the idlis under the seat and followed his friend upstairs to his room.

Once upstairs, Sheshu introduced Abhay to Ravi and Mohan. They offered Abhay some fruit juice to keep him occupied while they went to the kitchen to discuss what to do next. The three of them still needed to figure out the rest of their plan.

Meanwhile, back in the Modanis' home, Abhay's mother, Anuradha, had begun to wonder what was taking Abhay so long. He was usually back in half an hour. When she telephoned him, he said he would be back in five to ten minutes.

While he was on the phone with his mother, the three men decided to first tie Abhay up with the tape they had purchased earlier. As Abhay prepared to leave, Sheshu, Ravi and Mohan emerged from the kitchen. Sheshu calmly walked up to Abhay and told him he was being kidnapped.

Abhay burst into laughter, assuming it all to be a prank, but his mirth quickly faded when he saw Sheshu's unchanging expression and the roll of tape in his hands. Panic set in, and Abhay begged the three to let him go. The three would later tell the police that Abhay had pleaded with them, saying he had no money to give and that they should ask his father.

Sheshu took down the numbers of Abhay's father and other relatives. By now, Anuradha was in a state of full-blown panic and began calling her son's number over and over. Her frantic calls, however, only seemed to scare his kidnappers more and spur them on. As the calls kept coming in, the three men overpowered Abhay and tied his hands and legs together with his hands behind his back.

Terrified, Abhay began to scream for help, and the three decided they would have to tape his mouth shut lest someone came knocking on the door to make inquiries. They did so hurriedly before going to the kitchen to discuss their options.

Unbeknownst to the three kidnappers, Abhay was already gasping for breath in the other room. In their hurry, they had covered both Abhay's mouth and nose with duct tape. It was only a matter of a few seconds before he started to suffocate and collapsed on the floor. All life gradually ebbed out of his body and he was dead within minutes. In hindsight, the police later acknowledged that the three hadn't intended to kill Abhay.

Oblivious to the fact that Abhay was now lying dead on the floor in their house, Sheshu, Ravi and Mohan continued to discuss their plan. When they didn't hear any sound from the room for some time, Sheshu asked Mohan to go and check on Abhay. Mohan called out to him several times but the boy didn't respond. Mohan rushed back to the kitchen in a panic and told Sheshu and Ravi that their plan had gone horribly awry.

As the three men stood around Abhay's body, Sheshu was the first to react. He stuffed some newspaper in Abhay's nostrils before covering it with tape to prevent blood from oozing out, something he recalled from another movie he had seen in the past. Now in survival mode, Sheshu's next move was to switch off Abhay's mobile phone and get rid of any evidence that could incriminate them. He turned to Ravi and asked him to dispose of the phone far from the house and park Abhay's scooter elsewhere.

Ravi took the key and rode for about 5 kilometres. On the way, he tossed Abhay's phone and parked the scooter at Volga Hotel in an area called Darussalam.

By the time he returned, Sheshu and Mohan had procured a carton about 2 feet tall and 3 feet wide from a shop nearby to hide Abhay's body in. The three men cut the box in half and stuffed the body into it before covering it with a white plastic sack.

Sheshu's attention now turned to covering up their tracks. He went to his landlady, Sandhya Shivpurkar, and told her he would be moving out temporarily. He asked her for the document he had submitted as identity proof, saying he had been offered a job near Hyderabad Film City. He promised her he would be back in a month.

The three kidnappers then packed up all their belongings, changed their clothes and vacated their flat around 6.30 p.m., ensuring that they weren't seen leaving the building. They hailed passing vehicles and were relieved when a white Tata Ace, a mini-truck, stopped. They loaded their luggage and the carton containing Abhay's body into it and set out for the Secunderabad railway station. Sheshu told Ravi and Mohan to ride in the mini-truck while he followed in an autorickshaw.

On the way to the station, Sheshu thought of buying a different phone to avoid being tracked by the police. The mini-truck driver reluctantly stopped at Jagdish Market, where Sheshu sold Ravi's Celkon mobile phone for Rs 500 and used the money to buy a smaller, second-hand, dual-SIM phone for Rs 400.

While Sheshu was buying the phone, the driver of the mini-truck lost his patience and refused to wait any longer.

After an argument with Mohan and Ravi, he unloaded their bags and the carton on the road, took his payment and left.

The three then continued their journey in an autorickshaw. Once they reached the Secunderabad railway station, they discussed how to dispose of the carton as inconspicuously as possible. The three men set the carton down in front of Alpha Hotel, near a petrol station, and walked into the station.

Though their plan had taken a dark turn, Sheshu hadn't given up on their goal—a life-changing ransom. But first, they would need new SIM cards to continue with their plan. They went to a mobile store near the railway station and bought two preactivated SIM cards for Rs 200 each—four times the cost of a regular SIM card, but with the benefit of increased anonymity.

* * *

It had now been two hours since Abhay left the house, and Anuradha began to fear the worst. After alerting her sister-in-law, Kavita, who lived in the same house, she called her husband, Rajkumar, and told him that Abhay hadn't returned home. Like other residents of the neighbourhood, the Modanis belonged to the Marwari community and lived in a joint family.

Rajkumar was at work when he got the call from his worried wife. As he tried to wrap his head around the news, he telephoned his cousin Brijgopal Bhutada and a few relatives. Brijgopal said, 'He called me around 6 p.m. and said that Abhay had gone out to buy snacks two hours ago but had not returned home. He never stayed out for that long. He would either go to the tiffin centre and return within fifteen minutes or go to a friend's house within the colony. But that day they couldn't find him anywhere.'[4]

Brijgopal rushed to Rajkumar's place from his house in Banjara Hills. Notifying the police seemed like the most appropriate option, and together they went to Shah Inayat Gunj police station with a few other relatives. They reported the incident to the police, who registered the complaint as a kidnapping case around 8 p.m. Meanwhile, another group of relatives decided to check at the government hospitals nearby in case Abhay had met with an accident.

Soon after registering the complaint, a police team went to Mahalaxmi Tiffin Centre with a photograph of Abhay. 'We assumed that he was missing and started searching for him in the area. We had no idea that he was already dead,' said Rama. The police tracked Abhay's phone to Hindi Nagar and another team travelled there to widen the search.

Around this time, the Modanis got a call from Sheshu, who was about to board a train to Vijayawada along with Mohan and Ravi. Brijgopal said, 'Rajkumar's sister-in-law, Kavita, got a call around 10 p.m. The man on the other end said Abhay was with him and demanded a ransom of Rs 10 crore. Some of our relatives who were at home quickly brought the phone to the police station.'

Kavita's phone lacked a call-recording feature so the first thing the police did was to put her SIM in Brijgopal's phone. Then they told him to be ready to record the next call. They all waited at the police station.

The kidnapper called fifteen minutes later and Rajkumar answered the phone. On the police's instructions, he tried to

---

[4] From an interview with Brijgopal Bhutada in Hyderabad on 11 December 2017.

prolong the conversation as much as he could by bargaining with the kidnapper and giving the cops a chance to track his location or find any clues.

Kidnapper: I told you. You have to give Rs 10 crore.

Rajkumar: Rs 10 crore! Who is speaking?

Kidnapper: This is the kidnapper speaking.

Rajkumar: What enmity do you have with us?

Kidnapper: How much can you give?

Rajkumar: At this time, I have around Rs 5 lakh cash and 10–20 tolas (100–200 grams) of gold jewellery that belong to the ladies at home.

Kidnapper: Rs 5 crore is the last offer.

Rajkumar: I don't have that kind of money at home.

Kidnapper: Don't lie to me. Rs 5 crore is the final offer.

Rajkumar: Rs 5 crore is a huge amount. It'll fit in 5–7 large suitcases.

Kidnapper: Don't talk too much. Do whatever you need to do and get the money. Rs 5 crore is the last offer.[5]

Rajkumar continued to plead with the kidnapper but in vain. The kidnapper, who didn't speak Hindi fluently, told him he would get his son back at 6 a.m. the next day if he brought the money to the Secunderabad railway station.

While the police planned their next move, Rajkumar's relatives continued their search. Brijgopal said they formed five groups of two to three people each. 'The police were helpful.

---

[5] Excerpts of the phone conversation from the recording played on news channels. See https://www.youtube.com/watch?v=-hK3lntvKhk

A few officials went out in two jeeps to look for Abhay. But we wanted to help too. We searched all the surrounding areas, including Begum Bazaar, Kabutar Khana and Moazzam Jahi Market, updating each other through social media. We must have searched around half the city that night,' he said.

Meanwhile, word of Abhay's kidnapping reached senior police officials, including Mahender Reddy, the first police commissioner of Hyderabad since the creation of Telangana. Other senior officials, including Deputy Commissioner of Police A. Venkateshwar Rao, supervised the investigation.[6]

Rao deployed seven teams, each comprising a senior inspector, an inspector and half a dozen constables. He said, 'The teams divided up the work between them. They fanned out and began to pick up people for questioning.'

One team was tasked with questioning the parents and other relatives of the victim while another was put in charge of collecting physical evidence. A third was told to collect electronic evidence, including call records and CCTV camera footage from around the Modanis' home and Mahalaxmi Tiffin Centre. A fourth team was told to get the address to which the kidnapper's phone number was registered and verify it. 'We found out that the SIM card had been registered to an address in Musheerabad, but when we reached there, we realized it was a fake address,' said Inspector Ravinder Reddy. As per the usual protocol, apart from tracking the location of Abhay's mobile phone, the police also looked at the footage from the CCTV cameras installed near the Modani residence and Mahalaxmi Tiffin Centre.

---

[6] Interview with A. Venkateshwar Rao in Hyderabad on 11 December 2017.

A couple of hours after the complaint was registered, the team tasked with scanning the CCTV footage made the first breakthrough—they spotted Abhay riding pillion on a scooter with an unidentified man on Aghapura Road in Hindi Nagar, close to Sheshu's house. The police now had a suspect.

* * *

All this time, the carton containing Abhay's body had remained untouched near the Secunderabad railway station but had begun to draw the attention of workers at a nearby petrol station and passers-by. One of the employees at the petrol station informed the local police that a carton had been lying unclaimed near Alpha Hotel for many hours.

Taking no chances, the police called in the bomb squad. They examined the carton and declared it safe before proceeding to open it. Abhay's father and other relatives had by then reached the spot. Soon, their worst fears were confirmed. They realized that the kidnappers had killed Abhay long before they made the first ransom call.

Brijgopal said, 'Until the ransom call came, we thought that Abhay may have gone somewhere by himself and would return home. After the call, we believed that he was still alive. Why else would they demand a ransom? We were all confused. None of us had imagined that they would kill him.'

The police took Abhay's body to Gandhi Hospital for a post-mortem, which was conducted at 2.30 p.m. on 17 March. It revealed that while Abhay had died of asphyxiation, he had sustained several injuries before his death. He had bruises on his waist, nose and lower lip, and his trachea was filled with a 'blood-stained, frothy liquid'[7]. While doctors weren't able to ascertain the precise time of death, the report said that Abhay had died between twelve and twenty-four hours before the post-mortem was conducted.

The police now focused all their efforts on finding the kidnappers.

As Abhay's family mourned his loss, the kidnappers contacted Rajkumar for the third time in the early hours of 17 March, unaware that Abhay's body had been found. This time, they communicated using SMS, and sent Rajkumar instructions on how to send them the ransom. Rama said, 'Sheshu sent a text message to Rajkumar, instructing him to leave the money on a train to Bhubaneswar. We tracked the location of his phone and realized that he was on the move— on board a train to Vijayawada.'

Sheshu, however, had begun to suspect that Abhay's body had been found and that the police were tracking their movements using his phone. Trusting his gut, he threw the phone out of the train between the Yerrakata and Singinaru bridge. Unfortunately for him, a railway contract worker, G. Shivaparvati, found the phone while cleaning the tracks around noon on 17 March. She informed her supervisor, Krishnam Raju, who told the police. A few days later, Sheshu's discarded phone was in the hands of the police.

Having found a clue about the kidnappers' location, a team of policemen was dispatched to look for them along the railway tracks. By the time the police reached Vijayawada, however, the three men had boarded another train to Berhampur.

---

[7] *The State vs Indugamalli Sheshu Kumar, Pondara Ravi & Namburi Mohan*, Sessions Case No. 389 of 2016 (Court of the Metropolitan Sessions Judge, Hyderabad, 19 January 2018).

Back in Sree Colony, the entire neighbourhood was in a state of shock and grief over Abhay's death. The police circulated the picture of him on the scooter with the suspected kidnapper in the hope that someone would recognize the man. Police officers said that initially the aged gentleman whom Sheshu cared for couldn't identify him from the CCTV grab. No one from Abhay's family knew who he was. The police showed the photo to others in the neighbourhood and finally got a breakthrough when an eight-year-old girl said she recognized the man as Sheshu or 'Sai' as everyone called him. The police were able to get in touch with other members of the Darak family only after the girl identified him. 'We realized then that though Sheshu had spent time with children in the neighbourhood, none of their parents knew who he was, and few had even seen him,' said Ravinder.

The eight-year-old girl told the police that Sheshu used to work at the Daraks' home. Policemen visited them and soon had plenty of information about him. The Daraks also told them about the Kartikeya Foundation. Soon, the trail of breadcrumbs led the police to Sheshu's house in his home town of Rajahmundry in Andhra Pradesh.

Two days after Abhay's body had been found, a police team was sent to Rajahmundry, but they soon found that Sheshu hadn't been there recently. With Sheshu's identify confirmed, the police began to track his personal SIM card. Its last-known tower location was in Berhampur. Another police team was dispatched there and told to coordinate with the team in Rajahmundry.

But the three kidnappers were still a step ahead of the police.

* * *

When Sheshu, Ravi and Mohan arrived in Berhampur, they realized they were short on cash. They went to Ganesh Market, where they sold Sheshu's smartphone for Rs 2000. They then rented a room in Anarkali Lodge with the money. When they turned on the news on local TV channels, they quickly realized that the police were on their trail.

Knowing they would be caught if they stayed put, the three men left the lodge two days after they checked in. They decided to take their chances in Sheshu's home town and bought bus tickets to Rajahmundry. When the police arrived at the lodge, the manager confirmed that the three had spent a couple of nights there but had already checked out. 'We knew that Sheshu was from Rajahmundry and suspected that they would try to go there. We instructed the team that had been dispatched to Rajahmundry to stay put and search the area,' said Rama.

Sheshu, Ravi and Mohan reached Rajahmundry bus station and were trying to figure out their next move when they ran out of luck. Around 2 a.m. on 20 March, less than an hour after they were dropped off by the bus, six policemen apprehended them at the bus depot. They were escorted back to Hyderabad.

A day after the body was found, the news spread, and soon everyone in the city was talking about the brutal murder of a fourteen-year-old boy in broad daylight. After their arrest, Police Commissioner Mahender Reddy used his magisterial powers and invoked the Preventive Detention Act.[8] He ordered that the three accused be placed in police custody,

---

[8] In Hyderabad, if an individual is found to be involved in two or more criminal cases including petty crimes, the police commissioner may choose to invoke the Preventive Detention Act. If the commissioner feels that the accused person has

and as per the act, neither of them could apply for bail for a year. The three are currently lodged in the Hyderabad city jail in Chanchalguda.

Ravinder Reddy, inspector at Shah Inayat Gunj police station, took over from Rama after he was transferred, about a month and a half after the incident took place.[9] Rama had completed most of the investigation by then.

On 19 January 2018, less than two years after they were arrested, the Metropolitan Sessions Court in Nampally found Sheshu, Ravi and Mohan guilty of murder, kidnapping for ransom and other crimes, and sentenced them to life in jail.[10] It was a speedy trial by the standards of the Indian judiciary, even for a high-profile case, and the police attributed this to the abundance of physical evidence and strong witness statements. Among the forty-three police witnesses was Lalith Jain, owner of the shop Pushpa Laminates. The CCTV camera at his shop had recorded the three men leaving the building with the carton. Another witness was Mohd Tariq Siddiq, who saw Ravi parking Abhay's Honda Activa at Volga Hotel.

The police also collected CCTV footage from seventeen different locations. They found footage of Abhay entering the building near where Sheshu lived. In the footage from Pushpa Laminates, Abhay was seen alive for the last time when he entered the building. The same camera also recorded Sheshu

---

disrupted public tranquillity, the accused can be detained in police custody for up to a year without bail.

[9] From an interview with Ravinder Reddy (inspector) in Hyderabad on 8 December 2017.

[10] *The State vs Indugamalli Sheshu Kumar, Pondara Ravi & Namburi Mohan*, Sessions Case No. 389 of 2016 (Court of the Metropolitan Sessions Judge, Hyderabad, 19 January 2018).

parking the scooter as well as the three leaving the building with their bags and the carton wrapped in the white plastic sack.

Ravinder said, 'We sent samples of Sheshu's voice and the recording of the kidnapper's voice for analysis and found that they matched.' The police said they also found material evidence, including Abhay's glasses in the kidnappers' flat and his slippers in a bathroom on the building's ground floor. Apart from the camera near Sheshu's house, the police later also found footage that showed Ravi parking Abhay's scooter at the Volga Hotel.

Hyderabad has one of the country's most extensive networks of CCTV cameras, which were set up soon after the state of Telangana was carved out of Andhra Pradesh on 2 June 2014. Ravinder said that a month after the state was formed, the government decided to install cameras across the city for better surveillance. He added, 'We also encouraged the public to install CCTV cameras in their neighbourhoods. Since then, many housing societies have set up CCTV cameras. We now have at least 1 lakh such cameras in Hyderabad, which include those set up by the government and by citizens, and the police can monitor the entire network.'

* * *

The public prosecutor, also named P. Ravinder Reddy, asked for the death penalty for all three kidnappers, but the court decided to award them life sentences instead, noting that the case didn't fall into the 'rarest of rare' category, which is the Indian judiciary's benchmark for awarding the death penalty. Ravinder said factors such as the convicts' ages (all three were under twenty-five) and the fact that none had a history of crime may have contributed to the court's decision.[11]

Recounting the scene when the judge pronounced his verdict, Ravinder said, 'Rajkumar and his wife, Anuradha, were visibly relieved. All three convicts fell to their knees. The victim's father had been very closely involved in the trial, and when the judge sentenced the kidnappers to life, he said justice had been done. However, the three convicts pleaded with the judge, insisting they were innocent.'

The order given by the sessions court, however, is not the end of the road for Sheshu, Ravi and Mohan.[12] They can appeal the sessions court's judgment in the high court and the Supreme Court, but it has not been done yet.

Ravinder, the public prosecutor, however, is confident that even if they do appeal to the higher courts, because of the strong evidence, it is unlikely that the sessions court's decision will be overturned or their sentences reduced.

During the trial, neither of the accused was able to apply for bail even once as they could not afford to pay the surety amount of Rs 10,000. While Sheshu managed to find a lawyer for himself, the other two were too poor to do so and had to share a lawyer appointed on the court's directions from the state's Legal Aid Services.

The defence lawyers didn't call a single witness to refute the prosecution's case. They instead argued that the

---

[11] From an interview with P. Ravinder Reddy in Hyderabad on 8 December 2017.

[12] *The State vs Indugamalli Sheshu Kumar, Pondara Ravi & Namburi Mohan*, Sessions Case No. 389 of 2016 (Court of the Metropolitan Sessions Judge, Hyderabad, 19 January 2018).

prosecutors had failed to establish the chain of events necessary for proving the charges.

One of them, who did not wish to be named, said that the life sentences given to the three men were harsh as they were not career criminals and hadn't intended to kill Abhay—a fact that the police acknowledged. The lawyer said, 'When a life is lost, it is a human tendency to blame someone. Every accident is not an offence and every mistake is not a crime. Any crime needs to have motive, intention and preparation. What happened was a childish act, and even though people make mistakes, everyone should get a chance to reform as no one is born a criminal.'

The defence lawyer has encouraged the three of them to take the case to the high court. He added, 'The three should appeal the decision as in my opinion the prosecution failed to prove the charges against them. I hope they get a better outcome in the high court, where the quality of the evidence will be judged rather than the quantity.'

* * *

Originally from Nizamabad district in what is now Telangana, the Modanis moved to Hyderabad more than two decades ago. Theirs is a joint family, in which Rajkumar and his younger brother, Sanjay, live with their parents, wives and children under one roof. Sanjay and his wife, Kavita, have two children.

Though relieved to see that justice has been served, Rajkumar, Anuradha and Abhishek—Abhay's twin—remain deeply affected by his death. Rajkumar's cousin Brijgopal said, 'They used to be a family that got along with each other and everyone around them. But when Abhay died, they stopped going out.' Over the past year, he and other relatives have been trying to help them to heal. 'They are recovering slowly and have started going out more often. We are worried that Abhishek will suffer emotionally if they don't move on from this tragedy. But he has been very brave. Less than a week after his brother died, he wrote his board exams,' he added.

The impact of Abhay's death extended beyond his immediate family to the entire neighbourhood. The death came as a jolt to all the children in the neighbourhood who played with Abhay every evening. For many months after, other residents of Sree Colony exercised extreme caution while leaving their children alone at any time of the day.

A resident of the area who wished to remain anonymous said that after the incident, the housing society hired more security guards. Residents also asked the police for increased security, and to this day a police van is dispatched to the society at night.

Another neighbour, forty-one-year-old Archana Sarda, who has lived there for the past two decades, said that Abhay's death seemed to have changed the neighbourhood for good. 'This is mainly a residential area, and it was once considered safe. Children here would play outdoors till 10 p.m. But now no one steps out after dark. Abhay's death affected everyone, but especially the children, who all knew each other. Abhay and Abhishek used to play cricket and badminton with my nephew but Abhishek rarely comes out to play now,' she said.

She added, 'The Modanis have now started going out and meeting as a family again but it will be some time before things are back to the way they were. Anuradha used to visit the temple regularly but now she goes occasionally.'

Ironically, despite the changes and increased security, Sree Colony remains one of the few housing societies in Hyderabad that lacks CCTV cameras, which proved so crucial in bringing Abhay's kidnappers to justice.

* * *

Kidnapping cases are packed with suspense and emotions, the ingredients of a thriller. In Abhay's case, however, the plan to kidnap him was lifted straight out of the plot of a movie. While its resemblance to a film's plot made this story a unique addition to this book, certain facts of the case also make it one of the most tragic.

Unlike other cases in the book, the police investigation showed that killing Abhay was not a part of Sheshu's, Ravi's and Mohan's original plan. His death was the result of a miscalculated move on their part. What baffled me though is their good luck, which helped them leave their apartment with a body in a cardboard box, load it on to two vehicles and place it in front of a petrol station without attracting anyone's attention.

Truth be told, I wasn't happy about approaching Abhay's parents. I had been informed that they didn't wish to speak to me or anyone else from the media. But journalists, after all, are taught to fight the odds. However, Abhay's family stayed firm in their resolve to avoid the media entirely, and after two attempts, I chose to respect their decision.

6

Franshela Vaz, Mumbai

29 June 2015 was a busy Monday morning for Sherly Vaz, a mother of two. She made breakfast for eight-year-old Franshela and her two-year-old brother, Floyd, before packing their tiffins in time for them to catch their respective school buses.

Juggling tasks, she glanced up at the clock.

It read 8 a.m.

However, it was actually 7.35 a.m. Like in countless Indian households, the kitchen clock had been set to run ahead of time to ensure that the children were never late for school.

Sherly shifted her gaze to a piece of paper stuck to the wall.

'Floyd's pickup: 8 a.m.,' it read.

It had been more than a year since she underwent surgery to remove a tumour from her brain, but Sherly's memory still frequently deserted her. The piece of paper—her husband Francisco's idea—helped her remember the pickup and drop-off times for her children.

Franshela was in class VIII and Floyd was a nursery student at New Horizons Public School, a ten-minute drive from their home in Ekveera Darshan housing society at Airoli. Unlike Floyd, Franshela had to leave for school much later at noon.

'Franshela, wake up and brush your teeth,' Sherly yelled out before running down the stairs, Floyd in her arms, to be in time for the school bus.

After dodging her mother's wake-up summons for another hour, Franshela rolled out of bed and dragged herself to the bathroom. After bathing and brushing, she headed to the dining room for a bowl of Chocos, her favourite cereal, before getting dressed for school.

When the kitchen clock struck noon, Sherly called out to her daughter again. 'Franshela, come on. It's time to go. I am going out to pick up Floyd. Hurry up.' Franshela, a diligent student who never liked missing a day of school, put her shoes on, grabbed her bag and ran downstairs. As Franshela reached the gate, she saw Floyd getting off the school bus and noticed—not for the first time—that the water bottle he was carrying wasn't his. Floyd seemed to have developed a curious habit of bringing back other children's water bottles. Sherly picked up Floyd in her arms and said goodbye to her daughter.

After lunch, Sherly took her sleep-inducing medication for staving off severe headaches—a side effect of her surgery. As she drifted off to sleep, she remembered how Franshela had told her that after the procedure, she need not pick her up from the gate every day. She smiled to herself and decided to cook some bhajjias as a treat for her daughter, who would be home in a few hours.

'Franshela loved eating vada pav, samosa and other types of fried snacks after school. Sometimes she would pick it up from the shop near the entrance of the building on her way back home. On that day I thought of surprising her by making bhajjias at home and ordered 1 kilogram of besan,' Sherly said.

* * *

A little after 6 p.m., Sherly woke up with a start and immediately checked the time. Franshela's school ended at 5.30 p.m., but she wasn't home yet. Sherly's mother, eighty-year-old Elsy Quadros, who was staying with them as Sherly's husband was away on a business trip, had already started to panic. Her daughter tried to calm her down. 'She must be buying snacks downstairs. I'll go out and check,' she told her mother.

Sherly hurried outside but there was no sign of her daughter. Just as she was on the brink of panicking, another thought struck her: 'Maybe the bus is running late. Maybe the other children haven't reached home either.' She ran back inside and telephoned a few parents.

A few minutes later, she knew this much: Franshela was indeed on the bus, and her friends had all made it back home. She was gripped by a sickening realization. For the first time in her life, she didn't know where her daughter was.

She enlisted the help of a few friends to search the neighbourhood, but there was no sign of her daughter. A friend then accompanied Sherly to Rabale police station, where they registered a complaint. Because Franshela was a minor, the police were required to treat it as a kidnapping case. With the cops now involved, word spread quickly, and many of the Vazs' neighbours joined in the search for Franshela.

After spending an hour at the police station, a distraught Sherly returned home and tried to compose herself before telephoning her closest confidant, her elder sister Sophia Fonseca, with the terrible news. Sophia was also Franshela's godmother.

As soon as she put the phone down, Sophia informed her husband, Clarence Fonseca, and got dressed to leave for her sister's house. Franshela was five years old when Clarence and Sophia had got married. She had been the flower girl at their wedding.[1]

News soon reached the top brass of the police department. Navi Mumbai Police Commissioner K.L. Prasad, Deputy Commissioner of Police (Vashi) Sahaji Umap and Deputy Commissioner of Police (Commissioner's Office) Suresh Mengde[2] all rushed to the Vaz residence.

* * *

Meanwhile, at the Vaz residence, Sherly's relatives decided to search the neighbouring buildings. They scoured people's homes, water tanks and even gutters, but found no trace of the missing girl. No one, it seemed, had seen Franshela return from school. Desperate for leads of any kind, relatives and friends responded to several hoax sightings. When someone said they had seen a girl resembling Franshela standing alone outside D-Mart, a grocery store, a group of

---

[1] https://mumbaimirror.indiatimes.com/mumbai/cover-story/alcohol-temper-jealousy/articleshow/48013015.cms

[2] From an interview with Suresh Mengde in Mumbai on 6 November 2017.

friends rushed there but soon realized it was another wild goose chase.

* * *

Sherly and her husband both hail from Goa. Francisco, or Francis, as everyone calls him, was away on a business trip to the Netherlands when Franshela went missing. As part of his daily routine, Francis would call his wife every evening and speak to her and the children. On 29 June, however, relatives telephoned Francis and broke the news to him.

Unable to make sense of what had happened, he tried to speak to his wife, but she was in no condition to speak when she was handed the phone. A neighbour filled him in. Hoping for the best outcome, Francis's colleagues arranged for his flight ticket back to Mumbai. He took the night flight and arrived in the city on 30 June.

The minute Francis found out that his daughter was missing, he had a strong suspicion that the kidnapper was someone his daughter knew. 'I always taught my daughter not to talk to any strangers or take anything from them. I knew she would never readily go anywhere with a stranger. I told the police to question my relatives as well,' he said.

Later that night, after a preliminary search, a police team led by Abhay Kakad, the then head constable stationed at the local beat chowki, arrived at the Vaz residence to find out if they had any suspects in mind.[3] Sherly named three people—a childless woman who attended the same church

---

[3] From an interview with Abhay Kakad in Navi Mumbai on 18 May 2018.

as them, a fruit seller who was always quick to compliment Franshela and a carpenter they had hired recently.

Kakad and his colleagues followed up on the three leads but they all led to dead ends. Their next move was to question people in the neighbouring buildings. This was when they stumbled upon their first credible lead. Darian Fernando, a fifteen-year-old boy, told the cops that on the day Franshela disappeared, he was on his way to his tuition class when he saw her outside her home, talking to a middle-aged man before getting into the passenger seat of his car. The police also found out from the boy that it was a red car.

DCP Sahaji immediately instructed a team of policemen, who had already begun checking CCTV camera recordings on routes leading away from Franshela's home, to look for the footage of a red car with a young girl in the passenger seat.[4] Using the description given by the boy, the police prepared a sketch of the man. Considering the disturbed state of mind they were in at the time, neither Sherly nor Francis remember seeing the sketch now. Sherly said that she wasn't thinking straight at the time, and Francis only returned home the day after the sketch was made.

As the police continued to scour CCTV camera footage from three locations, they came across a red car driven by a man, with a young girl in the passenger seat. They tracked down the car's registered address. Sahaji said, 'We went to the house but soon found that the girl in the car was not Franshela and that the man was her father.' Over the next few days, the

---

[4] From an interview with Sahaji Umap in Mumbai on 6 November 2017.

police investigated three more similar leads but they all turned out to be children who were with their parents.

Sahaji began to think that perhaps the car wasn't red after all. 'The boy had said that it was a red car but he may have been mistaken. All this while we were only looking for red cars. I then asked my team to look for any car with a young girl in the passenger seat,' he said.

The police went back to sifting through CCTV footage, and this time noticed a grey Hyundai i10 with a young girl in the passenger seat. The footage was from the Airoli Toll Naka. DCP Sahaji said, 'As soon as we had the number plate, we ran it through our software and Clarence Fonseca's name popped up. For three days after Franshela was kidnapped, we had visited the area around the house and spoken to many family members, so I recognized his name instantly. I telephoned DCP Suresh and told him that we had found the girl,' he said.

Suresh already had his suspicions about Clarence. 'When we questioned Clarence and his wife separately, their stories about his whereabouts did not match, so we knew something was wrong,' he said. Two teams of policemen, one accompanied by Francis, set out in search of Clarence. One team went to his mother's home in Malad but did not find him there.

The second, after searching his car and the area around his building at Mira Road, finally apprehended Clarence at his home. On 2 July, around 7.30 p.m., Senior Inspector Maloji Shinde and four other officials from the second team went up to Clarence's fifth-floor apartment at Mira Road and rang the bell.[5] Clarence answered the door. According to Maloji,

5   From an interview with Maloji Shinde in Mumbai on 9 January 2018.

Clarence pretended to be clueless and made no attempt to flee. 'There was no tension on his face. He behaved as though guests had come to his home and denied knowing anything about the girl,' said Maloji.

Sahaji added, 'When we arrested him, he denied any involvement in the case. He started asking us why he was a suspect and what was the basis of the allegations against him.' The policemen showed Clarence and his wife the CCTV footage of him and Franshela in his car. 'He kept on denying that he knew where she was, but soon his wife took our side and started questioning him as well,' said Maloji.

Sahaji added, 'We asked him to accompany us to a highway police chowki near Ghodbunder Road for questioning.' On the way to the chowki, DCP Sahaji said Clarence confessed to Maloji that he had indeed kidnapped Franshela, but had left her in a forest. 'When he said that, we realized that something terrible had happened and we asked the girl's father to go home. But he had expected the worst the minute Clarence emerged as the prime suspect,' said Sahaji.

With little hope of finding Franshela alive, Maloji set out with Clarence in a police van. He soon realized, however, that he was being led on a wild goose chase. 'He was trying to confuse us by taking us to wrong locations. We stopped at several places before we decided to take him to the police chowki for further questioning,' said Maloji.

Again, Clarence protested his innocence. At one point, the police brought his wife to the station to get him to confess. 'His wife hit herself on the head repeatedly, asking him why he did it. We were concerned as it had been three days since the girl went missing. If her body was not found, it would be impossible to prove she had been murdered,' said Suresh.

But after sustained interrogation that lasted through the night, in the early hours of 3 July, Clarence finally confessed he had killed Franshela and dumped her body in a forest near Ghodbunder Road. According to sources, he did not confess willingly and was beaten by his interrogators for several hours before he confessed and revealed the location of the body. 'His wife cooperated with us and helped us threaten him with dire consequences, after which he confessed and agreed to show us the body,' said a police official, who did not wish to be named.

As the interrogation continued, the police came to know of how it all went down.[6]

At 5 p.m. on 29 June, Clarence allegedly arrived at the gate of Ekveera Darshan. He waited there until 5.30 p.m. and when Franshela's bus pulled up, called out to her as she alighted. 'Franshela, come here. Your mother is not at home. She's at my house and I've come to pick you up. Let's go,' he said.

Franshela had little reason to doubt Clarence, whom she saw at least once a week when he visited with his wife and their children. Throughout the car ride, she remained calm, possibly since she looked forward to playing with her cousins at Clarence's house in Mira Road, where she also expected to meet her mother.

Clarence then allegedly drove down Ghodbunder Road. He stopped the car at Gaimukh, a village near Retibunder, and pulled out a plastic bag. Before she could even react, he grabbed her and covered her head with it. She struggled and thrashed about but he held on tight, and soon her eight-year-

---

6   The sequence of events mentioned in the chapter is as narrated by various police officials. The case is currently under trial, and Clarence is yet to be proven guilty in court since the judgment is still pending.

old body went limp. The police estimated that Clarence killed her between 6.30 p.m. and 8.30 p.m. the same day she was kidnapped.

Despite his meticulous planning, Clarence began to panic at the sight of Franshela's dead body. The police investigation would later reveal that this was around the time his wife telephoned him and told him of their niece's disappearance.

He drove a little farther and decided to dispose of Franshela's body in a forest near the Thane creek. He took off her shirt—which bore the logo of her school—before placing her body on the ground and covering it with a large banner he found lying nearby. In his panic, he disposed of her shirt just a short distance from her body.

Franshela's body was found on 3 July around 10 metres from the main road. DCP Suresh said, 'We have strong evidence against Clarence. Apart from CCTV footage and witness statements, we also found his driving licence around 10 feet from Franshela's body.'

Though Franshela had been missing for four days, the police had hoped to find her alive. 'Up until we interrogated him [Clarence], we had thought that we would find her alive. We never expected that he would kill her, and that too in such a gruesome way,' said Sahaji.

The Rabale police formally arrested Clarence at 5.45 a.m. on 3 July and seized his car. He remains in judicial custody at Taloja jail in Thane. According to several policemen who were there, he didn't once show remorse for his actions—not even when he finally led the police to the spot where he had dumped his niece's body later that day.

* * *

After Clarence was arrested, many people confirmed they had seen him near the entrance of Ekveera Darshan on the day of the murder. These included an employee of Krishna Bengali Sweets, who said Clarence had bought samosas on 29 June, just before Franshela's school bus arrived.

Amid confusion and anger, Sherly remembered that Clarence's behaviour was seemingly odd from the minute he had walked into her house with his wife, Sophia, and their three children at 11.30 p.m. on 29 June.

Head Constable Kakad, who kept guard outside their building, also remembered that Clarence was acting suspiciously. 'He walked in with earphones on and wouldn't make eye contact with anyone. As soon as I saw him, I knew something was wrong about him. We had been questioning the family members, and our superiors (DCPs Sahaji and Suresh) ordered us to check his house,' he said.

Upon entering the Vaz residence on the third floor, Clarence headed straight to the bedroom and didn't speak to anyone for the rest of the night. Sherly recalled that Clarence had appeared anxious and avoided being seen by any journalists. Fighting back her tears, she added, 'The man who murdered my daughter slept in the drawing room of my house. He had no shame at all. Even after killing her, he had the audacity to come and live in our house and pretend to look for her as well.'

When Clarence entered the Vaz residence with Sophia and their children, Sherly had asked them what took them so long. Clarence had then claimed that a man had stolen a folder from the passenger seat of his car and that he had chased him to get it back. 'We later found out that he had put the folder along with Franshela's bag on the seat, and while tossing the bag out of the car after he killed her, he threw the folder out as well by mistake. After realizing this, he had gone back to the spot with a friend to retrieve it, which is why he had reached our house so late,' Sherly said.

She recalled the lengths to which Clarence went to avert suspicion and mislead the police. It was his idea, she realized later, to suggest that the police search the apartments of people in the society who were living on rent to lead them astray. The society guard was summoned and asked to produce a list of rented flats in the society. Armed with the list, Sherly and Sophia visited every flat on it, but to no avail. Clarence had managed to throw them off the scent until his luck ran out.

He taunted the constables posted at the entrance of Ekveera Darshan for not being able to find Franshela. He even offered to take care of any ransom demands, even though the family had received none.

If Clarence's behaviour that day appeared odd, it was stranger still the next morning. 'He woke up early the next day [30 June] and went home [in Mira Road] with two of his children. After an hour, he called Sophia many times, asking her to come back home immediately with their youngest child,' Sherly said.

Sophia, however, wanted to be there for her sister during her time of need. Sherly said, 'When I asked him on the phone to let her stay, he shouted at me. He called me brainless and insensitive, saying that Sophia was needed at home since the children wouldn't eat without her.' Sophia reluctantly went back home with her daughter.

* * *

Franshela's post-mortem report said she had died of 'throttling' but did not mention the time of death, stating only that her body had already started to decompose when it was found. 'We couldn't even see our daughter one last time before saying goodbye,' said Francis.

While most kidnappings in India are motivated by money, Franshela's was different. Clarence had never intended to demand a ransom. Driven by anger, he had always wanted to kill her, according to the police. So what was the source of the anger that motivated Clarence to kidnap and kill his own niece in cold blood? It was the girl's mother—Sherly Vaz.

Sherly said their relationship had begun on a sour note. 'On the day of the wedding, his mother had misbehaved with us. She asked all our family guests to move and make way for her guests. When I complained to Sophia about his mother, he got very angry with me,' said Sherly.[7]

Over the years, the enmity between the two exploded into open hostility. Sahaji said that Clarence and Sherly had had many differences and fought often. 'During one fight, Sherly told him he would die at sea and never come back. He said that she would die of her brain tumour,' he said, adding that Clarence felt humiliated and wanted to teach her a lesson.

Till date, Sherly believes that Clarence's anger was driven by insecurity. 'He is a petty man, and we never got along. He was always jealous of us even though he had a three-bedroom flat. He didn't want us to earn more than him. He didn't want me to conduct tuition classes, and he was very jealous

---

[7] From an interview with Sherly Vaz in Navi Mumbai on 26 October 2017.

of Francis's job, especially when he went abroad. Francis was trying to take us to the Netherlands with him, and Clarence didn't want this to happen. He took revenge by killing my innocent daughter,' she said.

Sherly also recalled that Clarence was very stern towards Franshela and that she was always scared of him. 'He would scold her for little things, even for not eating quickly enough,' she said.

Sherly no longer speaks to her sister even though she knows Sophia knew nothing about Clarence's plan. 'Clarence's mother, Sushila, and Sophia came to meet us after the funeral, but Francis and his brother insulted them and told them to leave. We never met her again,' Sherly said.

The last fight that Sherly can remember was on 21 May 2015 when she had gone to Clarence's house in Mira Road. 'It was our wedding anniversary, and Franshela and I had gone to Sophia's house. We had a petty fight about some story he made up. He claimed that I had asked his five-year-old son Karl to touch a glass of hot milk when nothing of that sort had happened. The fight escalated and Sophia got angry and left the house. We didn't speak to each other for quite some time after that,' she said.

The police claimed that Clarence's insecurity extended to his own wife as well. He was distrustful of her, especially when he was at sea. 'He installed cameras in the kitchen, the living room and the bedroom to make sure that she was not cheating on him,' Sherly said. A source in the police department confirmed that they had noticed the cameras.

Sophia, however, refuted the claims and said that the cameras had been installed for the safety of her children. 'Clarence was away at sea most of the time, and I had to take care of three children on my own. We had installed the cameras so that we could keep an eye on them,' she said.[8]

The awkwardness and the exchange of cold looks at Thane court is common between the members of Clarence's and Sherly's families. Clarence has the support of his family members who show up whenever he is produced in court. It is also the only time he is able to meet his three children, five-year-old Tamara, three-year-old Samara and seven-year-old Karl, one at a time.

A family member close to the Fonseca family who did not wish to be named said that Clarence was the youngest among his siblings, and was a dutiful son and a loving father to his children. Though the relative couldn't say if Clarence indeed had anything to do with the kidnapping and murder of Franshela, he did mention that the police had fabricated a lot of evidence to support their case, including claiming that his driving licence was found close to the body.

At the time, the media covered the case extensively, and members of the Fonseca family believe that there was a lot of pressure on the police to present a strong case. 'The police planted evidence to build their case. They prepared the statements and then asked the witnesses to come and sign on them,' said the relative.

* * *

In a brief meeting with Clarence, he alleged that the police had framed him for his niece's death and added that the real

---

[8]   From an interview with Sophia Fonseca and Clarence Fonseca in
       Mumbai on 13 July 2018.

culprit was still at large. Clarence, who was in the merchant navy, had returned home on 15 March and was scheduled to leave for an assignment in July, about a week before the incident took place.

Clarence blamed the police for planting evidence against him. He claimed that they could prove no clear motive behind the crime they were trying to pin on him. He reasoned that had he committed the murder, it made no sense for him to go back to Franshela's house later that day.

Sophia said that she had seen his driving licence in his wallet back at home after the police picked him up for questioning on 2 July. 'My husband's wallet was in his pants. After the police arrested Clarence, they asked me to remove the debit cards and cash but leave the wallet behind. At that time, I had seen my husband's driving licence in his wallet,' she said, adding that the police may have taken it after she left the house with her children.

Clarence's version of events on that day end on a different note. He claims that he had indeed gone to Sherly's house on 29 June, but to pick up his mother-in-law, Elsy, to take her back to his house. He had wanted to surprise his wife.

He was supposed to leave for his next assignment in another week or so, and he apparently wanted to bring Elsy back home early so that Sophia would have an extra hand to help take care of their children. When he reached the gate of Ekveera Darshan, Clarence claims that he spotted Franshela as she alighted from her school bus. 'She saw me and insisted on going for a joyride in my car. So I took her around for fifteen to twenty minutes and then dropped her back home. After she went into the building, I left. I don't know who took her afterwards,' he said.

Clarence also alleged that during the interrogation, the police had beaten him up badly and threatened to hurt his daughter if he didn't confess to killing Franshela. 'If you threaten me with my child's safety at stake, which parent won't agree to anything?' he asked, implying that the police had forced a confession out of him.

His advocate, Gajanan Chavan, said that the behaviour of the police towards Clarence, who was left limping after his arrest, was questionable and he would bring it up in the trial. Before he was able to find a defence lawyer to represent him in the trial, Clarence had filed an application for bail while he was in judicial custody, but he didn't get any relief from the court.

No matter the verdict, Sophia's world has been shaken. Being Franshela's godmother, Sophia had shared a close bond with her niece as well as her sister, Sherly. 'My husband is in prison, my god-daughter is dead and my sister no longer speaks to me. I don't know who is telling the truth and whose side I should be on. I have lost so much, and I dread the day I'll have to stand in the witness box,' she said.

Life as a single parent hasn't been easy for her, and she is still learning how to manage. She now teaches the kindergarten class at St Aloysius School in Bandra where she has enrolled all three of her children. After Franshela's death, she lost her biggest support, Sherly and her family. She now has to take care of her children by herself, with some help from her neighbours.

Despite her tricky predicament, Sophia said that Clarence had never been violent towards either Franshela or Floyd. 'He was a concerned parent and would put his own children's interests before anyone else's. But he was good to his niece and nephew,' she said.

* * *

For months after Franshela's death, no one in the Vaz household spoke much. Her brother, Floyd, who was just two when she was kidnapped and killed, and knew nothing about her gruesome death, would console Sherly when she broke down, telling her that Franshela would return from school soon.

Francis and Sherly remember their daughter as a loving child who was very protective of her brother. 'She was interested in photography and loved taking pictures with the phone. She was very bright and loved being read to every night. She wouldn't sleep until I had read a story to her. Now Floyd has picked up her habit and refuses to sleep without a story,' said Sherly.

Though the pain of losing their daughter remains, the family is trying to lead a normal life. Francis has started travelling again for official assignments. Floyd is now in school. Francis and Sherly plan to stay in Mumbai until the trial is over, after which they plan to move back to Goa to start life afresh.

More than three years after Franshela's death, the case finally came up for trial at the Thane District Sessions Court at the end of June 2018, and the prosecution is yet to prove the allegations against Clarence in court. The police submitted the charge sheet to the court on 28 September 2015.

Officials at Rabale police station said that the major hold-up was that the analysis of the CCTV footage had been sent to the Forensic Science Laboratory (FSL) at Kalina, Mumbai. The lack of infrastructure and manpower at FSL is responsible for holding up many cases that rely on forensic evidence. The trial, however, is inching along.

Francisco and Sherly have just one wish—a speedy trial and severe punishment for the accused. Even though the trial has finally started, Sherly struggles to understand the lengthy legal process. 'Clarence is a criminal and should get the death sentence. But no matter what punishment he gets, we will never get our daughter back. When the police have evidence against him and we all know that he has done it, why do we have to wait for years to get justice?'

Today, years after Franshela was abducted and murdered, a lone CCTV camera watches over the spot from where her uncle kidnapped her.

* * *

Of all the cases, this is the only one I had written about at the time of the incident. The first messages that were forwarded on various WhatsApp groups stated that an eight-year-old girl had gone missing, that she hadn't returned home from school. I recall wondering whether she may have run away from home after a fight she had at home. The possibilities were endless.

We all expected another message later which read that the police had found her and that she had been reunited with her family. But the following day, reporters realized that the matter was more serious than that. Once her body was found, journalists from every newspaper and news channel thronged Ekveera Darshan in Airoli. I was one of them.

None of us, however, were allowed to enter by the police who had been stationed at the entrance of the building after some television journalists tried to speak to the family. With the help of a sympathetic staff member of New Horizons Public School, I managed to walk past the policemen, posing as one of the teachers who had come to offer their condolences to the Vaz family.

When I entered their flat, the first person I saw was Franshela's mother, Sherly. She sat on a chair holding her son, Floyd, who was two years old at the time. She broke down several times as people tried to console her, and I remember her saying, 'Whom can we really trust when the man who killed her was living in my house?'

Not only did Sherly and Francisco lose their daughter, they also have to face their close relatives at every hearing of a lengthy trial. While the case is pending in court, the incident has permanently altered the dynamics of Sherly's relationship with her sister, Sophia.

While reminiscing about happier times, Sherly always has an anecdote about Franshela to share. Despite all that happened, it's good to see that Sherly hasn't lost her warm and friendly nature, a trait most people said Franshela was known for.

7

Yash Lakhotia, Howrah

Subhash Kumar Sultania's phone rang at 6 a.m. on 31 January. Groggily he answered the call from an unknown number. What the caller told him banished all sleep. The body of a child had been found on Foreshore Road. It more or less fit the description of a boy Subhash had been looking for.[1]

His first call was to Anil Lakhotia, the father of the missing boy, Yash. Subhash told him about the body that had been found behind some bushes. He and others had spent the last two days searching for seven-year-old Yash. All the while, Anil had tried to suppress the persistent, unbearable thought that his son may have been killed. He hoped the body wasn't his son's, and asked Subhash, who was a close friend, to go check.[2]

Praying that the caller had been mistaken, Subhash got out of bed and quickly got dressed. Foreshore Road was less than 500 metres from his house, and he was there in ten minutes.

---

[1] From an interview with Subhash Kumar Sultania in Kolkata on 8 June 2018.

[2] From an interview with Anil Lakhotia in Kolkata on 15 February 2018.

On his way, Subhash made a second call, to Shibpur police station, and told them about the body. When he got there, he saw a few people standing around the body of a young boy in a school uniform. There was blood oozing from his nose and mouth, and a blackish mark half an inch thick around the boy's neck, indicating that he may have been strangled.

Subhash, however, couldn't be sure if the body was indeed Yash's. He telephoned Anil again to check two things: Did the boy have protruding teeth and a surgical scar on his stomach? Yash had had surgery to remove a cyst in his stomach when he was five years old.

Subhash confirmed both marks. On the other end of the call, Anil knew he had nothing left to hold on to. It was time to accept the unbearable thought that had haunted him for the past forty-eight hours: his seven-year-old son had been kidnapped, murdered and dumped by the roadside.

* * *

The Lakhotias were a joint family, originally from Sikar district in Rajasthan, who had been living in Kolkata for three generations. Anil owned a well-known sweet shop called Panch Bhog, and Yash's uncle, Nandkishore Lakhotia, was a property dealer.

In 2009, when Yash went missing, social media wasn't as popular as it is today. Many people had read or heard about Yash's disappearance in the newspapers and news channels, while others had come to know of it through word of mouth.

Yash had been kidnapped from his school, M.C. Kejriwal Vidyapeeth School in Liluah. Unlike the many cases where kidnappers pick up victims from a spot close to their homes,

Yash was picked up from school just before the van arrived to take him home.

A class II student, Yash was a friendly, talkative boy. Since the school he attended did not have buses, the parents had arranged a van to take their children to and from school every day. On 29 January, the van arrived at the Lakhotias' home on G.T. Road at the usual time, 7 a.m., to take Yash to school.

Later that day, when it was time for him to return and there was no sign of him, by 2.15 p.m., Anita, Yash's mother, began to get restless. The van that usually dropped Yash off at 2 p.m. every day hadn't arrived yet. She asked Anil, who was home for lunch, to make some calls. Though concerned, Anil and Anita weren't alarmed. The driver was sometimes late and on two occasions, had left Yash behind at the school by mistake.

Anil telephoned the owner of the van service, Hemant Sharma, to ask about his son's whereabouts. After a quick phone call to the driver, Dharam Raut, Hemant told Anil that Yash hadn't boarded the van. He wasn't around when the driver went to pick up the children after school. Anil's pulse quickened. He asked Hemant to check whether his driver knew why Yash hadn't been at the stop.

When Hemant called him back, the colour drained from Anil's face. 'Hemant said the van had broken down on the way to the school and had reached there ten minutes late. Yash wasn't there. He assumed our personal driver had picked him up,' he told Anita. This wasn't possible because Anil hadn't sent anyone to pick Yash up. 'Whenever we did so, we would inform him and the school well in advance. We couldn't imagine what had happened as the school wouldn't have allowed Yash to leave with a stranger,' said Anil.

Anil alerted his family members before rushing out
of the house. He reached the school around 3.30 p.m. and
went to meet Mallika Mukherjee, the then headmistress. She
immediately ordered a thorough search of the school premises
to ensure that Yash hadn't fallen asleep or hurt himself. While
school employees began scouring the premises, Anil and his
relatives began to look for Yash around the school.

There was no sign of the boy anywhere, so Mallika began
to ask around to find who had last seen him. She summoned
Binita Dubey, Yash's class teacher, who was in charge of
releasing the students that day. The school's policy stated
that students had to identify the person with whom they were
going home before the teacher allowed them to leave. In the
statement she later gave to the police, Binita said she was with
the students when school hours ended at 1.30 p.m. Yash, she
said, told her that his uncle had come to take him home, but
she admitted she had not actually seen this 'uncle'.

In fact, nobody had. A few of his friends corroborated
Binita's story—that Yash had mentioned that an uncle had
come to pick him up. These included Sagnik Ghosh, a
classmate, who recalled that Yash mentioned this detail when
he said goodbye to him. But no one had seen him leave the
school with anyone.

By now, Anil was certain his son had been kidnapped.
He and his relatives went to Bally police station around 3.30
p.m. to file a missing-person complaint. But the distraught
family was in for another shock. Anil tried to explain to the
police that his son, by all accounts, had left the school with an
unknown person. The cops, however, were reluctant to register
a complaint. Instead, they tried to convince Anil that perhaps
his son had gone to a friend's house. 'When we told the police
that our child had been kidnapped, their response was to ask

us how we knew this. We explained that Yash was only seven years old and wouldn't go to a friend's house without telling us. But they simply wouldn't take us seriously,' said Anil.

A few phone calls to senior police officials in Howrah finally did the trick, and the Bally police finally registered the family's complaint around 5 p.m. As the police began their investigation, they sent a few cops to Anil's house to question his relatives and neighbours. Soon after the police reached the Lakhotias' home, news of the kidnapping spread quickly and was on television later that day.

Having informed the police, all Anil and his relatives could do was wait. Anil and his elder brother, Nandkishore, pinned their hopes on a ransom call and stayed up all night waiting for it. But no call came that day, or the next.

The police, meanwhile, were yet to find a promising lead. While questioning Yash's family, they asked Anil if he had reason to suspect someone he knew. After giving it some thought, Anil could think of only one name—Santosh Singh. Santosh, he told the police, was an acquaintance of Nandkishore who helped him in his real estate business.

Santosh was forty-seven, and Anil had known his family for more than a decade. Despite this, the two had never been on good terms. Anil saw him as a freeloader. 'He visited our sweet shop often. I never liked his habit of demanding sweets free of cost. We'd had several arguments about this. It was one of the reasons why we never got along,' said Anil. He added that he had once heard that Santosh had been involved in a kidnapping in Bihar.

When Anil mentioned Santosh to his family, more suspicious details emerged. His wife, Anita, said that Santosh had visited their home just a few weeks ago, on 25 December, when neither Anil nor Nandkishore were around. Recalling what his wife had told him, Anil said, 'He gave Yash a toffee before he asked him a few questions. After he left, my wife asked Yash what they had talked about. He told her that Santosh had asked him about his school timings.'

This was enough to convince Anil that Santosh was his son's kidnapper. He told the police about his suspicion and tried to find out about Santosh's whereabouts from his brother-in-law, Ganesh Chaudhary, who worked at his sweet shop. Anil recalled that just a day before the kidnapping, he had received a call from Ganesh telling him that Santosh had asked for 4 kilograms of sweets. Anil refused to give him any more sweets for free and told Ganesh to deduct the cost from his salary.

Ganesh told Anil that on 28 January he received a phone call from Santosh. He said he was going out of town and asked him to come to Howrah railway station with the boxes of sweets. Ganesh met Santosh outside the railway station and, as instructed, handed over the boxes to him at the entrance gate and left.

Both Anil and Nandkishore believed that Santosh had called Ganesh to the railway station only to create an alibi for himself. 'He wanted to make it seem as though he was leaving the city. It is really strange since he did not call Ganesh directly to the train to drop off the sweets but instead met him outside the station,' said Nandkishore. But the larger reason behind their suspicions was Santosh's difficult financial situation.

Senior police officials who were monitoring the investigation advised Nandkishore to telephone Santosh to find out more. Nandkishore duly called Santosh in the evening on 29 January. After exchanging pleasantries, Nandkishore asked him where he was, to which he replied that he was on his way to his home town of Hajipur. He also said he had heard about Yash's kidnapping and expressed sympathy. 'I asked him to come back and help us as he knew many people in the area. But he refused to do so. Any well-wisher would have returned to help us look for Yash,' Nandkishore said.

Meanwhile, the media's coverage of Yash's disappearance continued. It wasn't long before journalists discovered the identity of the first suspect. Before long, Santosh saw his name on the news channels and telephoned Nandkishore, asking why he was being considered a suspect. Hoping to persuade him to show up in front of the police, Nandkishore asked him to return to Howrah and sort out the 'confusion'. But he failed to convince Santosh, who quickly disconnected the call.

The Lakhotias spent the next day in a state of anxiety, hoping that the police would be able to track down Santosh and bring Yash back home. But the police didn't have much luck finding new leads. On the evening of 30 January, they asked Nandkishore to contact Santosh again, this time to get the message across that the family was willing to pay a ransom. 'We tried to offer him money indirectly. We told him that if he knew the person who had kidnapped Yash, he should convey to him that we are willing to pay any ransom,' said Nandkishore.

Santosh, however, understood the implication. The tone of his voice changed at once. 'He was angry about being implicated in the case. He simply said, "Now we'll see what happens" and hung up,' said Nandkishore.

Anil and Nandkishore held out hope for a ransom call. They lay awake that night discussing how much money they would need and how they would arrange for it. As dawn broke, they visited several temples to pray for Yash's safe return.

It was on the morning of 31 January that their phone rang. Anil, who was having a bath, rushed out in a towel to answer what he hoped would be a ransom call. He was surprised, however, to hear the voice of his friend Subhash instead, who told him that the body of a young boy, around Yash's age, had been found on Foreshore Road. His heart sank.

* * *

While Yash's school fell under the jurisdiction of Bally police station, the Lakhotias' home was under the Howrah police station's purview, and the place where Yash's body was found was under Shibpur police station. This led to considerable confusion about the jurisdiction. Eventually, Bally police took charge of the investigation, with Shankar Roychowdhury being the leading officer.

After the body was found, the police continued their investigation. They recorded Ganesh's statement on 1 February 2009 and then arrested him for alleged involvement in Yash's kidnapping. After interrogating him, Shankar said, the cops conducted a raid in Bihar, hoping to find Santosh. But he wasn't there. On 6 February the police arrested another suspect, van driver Dharam Raut.

To date, Anil firmly believes that the kidnappers would have made a ransom call had the media not covered the kidnapping in such detail. More than this, however, he blames his son's death on the police's poor handling of the case. 'From the moment we reported the crime to the police until the CID took over the investigation, the case was handled very poorly. The police had no idea about how to go about looking for my son. His body was found just a couple of kilometres from our house. It is still painful to think about it, as our son was so close to our house the whole time,' he said.

He said the police chose a wait-and-watch approach and wasted precious time questioning children at M.C. Kejriwal Vidyapeeth. He also said that instead of trying to find Santosh, the police simply advised him to wait for a ransom call. 'They told us to pay the ransom and get our son back first. Only then, they said, would they see about catching him,' said Anil. He said that at one point, when the police suspected that Santosh was in Hajipur, they asked him to send one of his workers there to confirm this instead of going there themselves.

Expressing incredulity, Nandkishore said that not only did the police fail to find Yash alive, they weren't even able to find his body. 'It was us who told the police that Yash's body had been found. They didn't make any effort to collect evidence or even cordon off the area where the body was found before taking it to the police station. They even forgot to shoot a video of the area where Yash's body was found and took the one we had shot,' said Nandkishore.

Subhash, too, recalled the police's incompetence on the day the body was found. He said that though he had told the police that Yash's body had been found, they made no arrangements to transport it to a mortuary. When the police finally arrived, he said, they were reluctant to touch Yash's body, leaving Subhash to pick it up and place it in their van.

Once they reached the police station, the body was placed on a table. The police needed a sniffer dog to recover evidence, and after many phone calls, they managed to find one that belonged to the railway police. When the dog was brought in, it almost attacked Subhash. 'The dog smelt Yash's body on the table and in an instant leapt on me since I was the only person in the room who had carried Yash's body. I was terrified that the dog would injure me. The police eventually brought him under control and he led them to Shibpur Ghat, where they found Yash's school bag,' he said.

The post-mortem examination of Yash's body was conducted by Dr Harashit Sarkar. His report stated that Yash's death was a homicide. He had been strangled to death with a nylon rope. Apart from the mark around his neck, his body bore several other injuries. He had bled from the mouth and nose, and suffered a fracture to his hyoid bone (below the jaw, at the root of the tongue). The report also stated that there was no food or water in Yash's stomach, which indicated that his kidnappers hadn't given him anything to eat or drink. Judging by the state of the body, the report stated, Yash had been killed on the night of 30 January.

Despite their efforts, the police failed to find Santosh, and in March 2009, the Criminal Investigation Department (CID) took over the case. It was a relief for the family. Both the police and the CID, however, had one suspect alone—Santosh Singh. But even after the case was transferred to the CID, there was no progress, until Sandip Ganguly, from the homicide department, was given charge of the investigation on 18 November 2009.

Five months after he took over the investigation, Sandip said that he got to know that Santosh had been implicated in another case by the Jadavpur police, who had accused him of carrying illegal arms. This case was also transferred to the CID, and another team of officials tracked him down and arrested him in April 2010. Sandip found out that Santosh had been lodged at the Presidency Correctional Home in Alipore. He went there to interrogate him over Yash's kidnapping and murder case.

On 5 May 2010, at the end of the interrogation, CID officials claimed Santosh had confessed to having kidnapped and murdered the seven-year-old boy. But to prove this in court, Sandip and his team needed concrete evidence.[3] On 11 May, the court remanded Santosh in police custody for twelve days. Sandip continued interrogating him in the hope that he would reveal more details about the crime. Santosh told him that after kidnapping Yash, he had kept the boy at Kishori Oil Mill near Foreshore Road. The mill had been closed for more than a decade.

While there, Santosh allegedly gave Yash a white T-shirt to wear instead of his school shirt, which he buried in a pit used to store oil cakes, the residue from the extraction of oil from mustard seeds. On 19 May 2010, the CID claimed, Santosh led them to the mill and used a shovel to dig up the buried shirt.

Sandip said the oil-stained shirt was once off-white with grey borders on the sleeves and had a pocket with the emblem of Yash's school. It also had a label that read 'Pratap Dresses', the shop from where Yash's parents had bought his uniform.

A CID official, who did not wish to be named, said that Santosh frequented the abandoned mill with his friends. They learnt that Mohanlal Ojha, a guard who lived alone at the mill, had been murdered in May 2009, just a few months after Yash. The CID took charge of this case as well, and soon charged Santosh with Mohanlal's murder too.

***

Considering that neither the police nor the CID had found anyone who said they had seen the person Yash had left school

---

[3] According to the court order *State vs Santosh Singh*, Sessions Trial Case No. 277 of 2010 (Court of Additional District and Sessions Judge, Howrah, 22 December 2014).

with, the boy's shirt became their main physical evidence. The police's theory was that there was long-standing hostility between Santosh and the Lakhotias, which led to Santosh deciding to kidnap Yash to get back at them. 'The family as well as the workers at their sweet shop said that Santosh had a habit of taking sweets without paying for them. Anil disliked Santosh and had once humiliated him at his shop to teach him a lesson,' said an official from the CID who requested anonymity.

The police also told a reporter for the *Telegraph* that Santosh had been demanding large sums of money from the Lakhotias for helping them in their business. The family, however, refused to pay him. This, the cops said, increased the bitterness between the two parties and prompted Santosh to plot revenge by kidnapping and killing Yash.[4]

When he was apprehended, Santosh told CID officers what he had told Nandkishore: that he had gone to his village in Bihar to attend a niece's wedding. He even provided pictures and videos from the function. A CID official, however, said that Santosh himself was in none of the pictures or videos.

The police had tried to track his tower location, but the CID officials claimed that the records showed his movement till Liluah and then stopped, possibly because he may have switched off his phone. He added that even the train ticket Santosh had produced to prove that he took a train out of the city a day before the incident was a general unreserved ticket, and the CID officials had no way to determine whether he had actually boarded the train or not.

* * *

4 https://www.telegraphindia.com/1090201/jsp/frontpage/
   story_10469408.jsp

On 11 May 2012, the CID charged Santosh with the kidnapping and murder of Yash. What followed was a two-year trial in the sessions court. The prosecution called in fifty witnesses while the defence produced none.

Apart from Anil, advocates Arabinda Naskar and Keya Ghosh, who represented the prosecution, also criticized the investigation that was carried out in part by the police and then the CID. 'The evidence that the police put up was weak. The investigation had a lot of flaws, and the CID didn't include a lot of evidence. Naturally, the defence counsel targeted these loopholes,' said Keya.[5] The defence stand was first taken up by Anand Sinha and thereafter by Dibyajyoti Singharay.

For instance, the post-mortem report had stated that Yash had been strangled using a nylon rope. Even though Dr Harashit, in his statement, had mentioned that he had collected and sent the nylon rope that was used to strangle Yash to the FSL for examination, it was never presented as evidence. 'The nylon string was a vital piece of evidence in the case. But the police were careless and never used it as evidence. Where did it go then?' asked Keya. The rope is not mentioned in the list of articles that were seized during investigation.

Doubt was also raised about Yash's school shirt recovered from Kishori Oil Mill, the only evidence that incriminated Santosh. Yash's mother, Anita, said that on 29 January, her son had left the house wearing a light-grey shirt, which was part of the school uniform. But when the CID officials found the shirt, they described the colour as off-white with grey coloured sleeves and it had a tailor mark of Pratap Dresses. The

---

[5] From an interview with Keya Ghosh in Kolkata on 16 February 2018.

defence advocate challenged the credibility of this evidence and claimed that the shirt could not be treated as evidence since Yash was not wearing the shirt that was recovered.

During his cross-examination by the defence counsel, Sandip said that after the recovery of the shirt, he didn't interrogate the parents about the school uniform. He didn't question the tailor or the owner of Pratap Dresses to confirm whether the shirt was indeed theirs. Anil, however, claimed that there was no doubt that it belonged to his son, and his wife, Anita, had clearly identified the shirt in court.

The judge eventually decided that the colour of the shirt could not be ascertained. 'The shirt the CID found was the same light-grey shirt that Yash wore. The defence lawyers simply wanted to create confusion around the colour so that the evidence could be discredited,' Anil said.

The defence brought up the statement of Babban Sharma, the manager of Kishori Oil Mill, and argued that the recovery of the shirt by the CID seemed suspicious. Referring to Babban's statement, he said it was fishy that around four CID officials had visited the mill to inquire about the guard Mohanlal's murder, three days before they took Santosh there on 19 May 2010, implying that they may have planted evidence.

When asked about the visit, the CID official said that Santosh had told them that he had kept Yash in an abandoned mill. But the area had many abandoned godowns, and it would have been difficult to find that particular mill before they took Santosh to the spot. 'We tracked down the owner of the mill and eventually found Babban who told us about the guard's murder. That day we asked him to be available with keys on 19 May 2010, when we took Santosh to recover the shirt,' he said.

When the CID officials questioned Santosh about it, he allegedly confessed that he had killed Mohanlal since he feared he would give him away. The trial of Mohanlal's murder case is still under way.

The list of loopholes didn't end there. While one theory was that Yash had left with his 'uncle' before walking out of school, Shubham Bhajoria, one of Yash's classmates, provided information that led to another theory. He told the police that while he was passing through Rameshwar Malia Lane on his way home, he had seen Yash in his school uniform around 2 p.m. getting into a red Maruti van. He added that there were three or four men in the vehicle, but he didn't see any of their faces. The police never found the van.

While Keya later said that Shubham's statement proved to be a disadvantage to the prosecution's case, Anil feels that Shubham may not have seen Yash that day. 'Rameshwar Malia Lane is just a couple of minutes away from our house. It doesn't make any sense to me that the kidnappers would bring Yash so close to our home after kidnapping him,' he said. However, Shubham's statement created confusion about the place from where Yash was kidnapped.

The case was further weakened by the witnesses who were reluctant to testify against Santosh, given his criminal history. 'Some of the witnesses were small children, and they were too scared to speak in court. Even the workers at the sweet shop refused to speak against Santosh out of fear,' said Keya.

One thing that both Keya and the CID official felt certain about was that Santosh couldn't have committed the crime alone and there were definitely other people involved. 'We had learnt from sources that a relative who was close to the family was part of the planning, but we weren't able to verify the person's involvement. Without witnesses, the charge of criminal conspiracy is difficult to prove,' said the CID official.

Dibyajyoti Singharay was the second advocate to represent Santosh, and he took over the case about a year before the last judgment was pronounced at the Additional Sessions Judge Court (5th Court, Howrah). By the time Dibyajyoti started appearing for the hearings, around eighteen witnesses had already been examined. He still maintains that the police and the CID had simply concocted a story to frame Santosh in the case without any evidence.[6]

Defending his stand that Santosh had nothing to do with Yash's kidnapping or murder, Dibyajyoti alleged that the police had failed to investigate the case properly and didn't look into the close relatives of the family as possible suspects. 'Yash didn't know Santosh well enough to leave school with him. Moreover, during the two days that he was missing, the family didn't receive any ransom call. Yash was kidnapped because of personal vendetta, and a close relative was behind it,' he said.

He highlighted the school's role in ensuring a safe environment for their students and stated that in this case, M.C. Kejriwal Vidyapeeth should have been held responsible for allowing Yash to leave with anyone apart from his parents. He added that the school was let off by the police and the blame was simply shifted to Santosh.

In the trial, Dibyajyoti also questioned the authenticity of the video recording the CID had presented of the recovery of the shirt that Santosh had supposedly led them to. He argued that the video had several gaps, and beyond a point, the time

---

[6] From an interview with Dibyajyoti Singharay in Kolkata on 16 June 2018.

didn't appear in the recording, which indicated that it had been tampered with. He added that Santosh's face was not visible in the video at all, and the CID had not collected the audio dialogue transcription either. During the trial, Santosh told the court that he had been threatened and physically assaulted by the CID officials. He also claimed that the recovery of the shirt had been done under coercion.

On 22 December 2014, the final judgment was pronounced by Nabanita Ray, the additional sessions judge, and Santosh was acquitted of all the charges. That day, the courtroom was packed with more people than usual, mostly journalists. While most of the people in the courtroom reacted with disappointment, Keya distinctly recalls the look of surprise followed by relief on Santosh's face the moment the judge announced his acquittal.

The judges attributed the acquittal to flawed evidence and 'glaring discrepancies' in the prosecution's case. She noted that the statements of the witnesses only indicated that Santosh was a regular visitor at Anil's sweet shop and that he had visited Anil's home on 25 December 2008. Santosh's location could not be ascertained based on his mobile network, nor was there any evidence regarding his whereabouts around the time Yash was kidnapped. Nabanita also mentioned that the police as well as the CID had not established the motive of the crime.

The CID and the police had also failed to prove Santosh's movement from Howrah to Bihar during or after Yash's kidnapping. She noted that the mobile phones belonging to Anil, Nandkishore and Santosh were not seized for examination of call records or to ascertain Santosh's location.

Despite being acquitted in Yash's case, Santosh's days of appearing in court are far from over. He is facing criminal charges in two other cases, including the murder of Mohanlal, and Dibyajyoti is representing him in both the cases. Santosh currently lives in Howrah with his family and continues to work in the construction business.

* * *

The brutal manner of Yash's death not only impacted his family but also his classmates, teachers and other members of his school. Kishan Kejriwal, the trustee of the twenty-year-old M.C. Kejriwal Vidyapeeth, said that Yash's teachers remember him as a cheerful and bright student.[7]

Kishan recalled that Yash's kidnapping had taken place just a couple of days before CCTV cameras were installed in and around the school premises, which could have otherwise helped identify the person Yash left with that day. 'We had already placed the quotation for the order for CCTV cameras, and in the next two or three days, the cameras were up and functional. Due to the lax behaviour of workers, the installation was delayed by a couple of days, which is really unfortunate,' Kishan said.

Following the incident, the school management made some changes to its policy of releasing students. Kishan said that the school started the system of escort cards for students of up to class IV. As per the new system, parents or guardians coming to pick up the students would have to show the escort card before the teacher allowed them to take the child.

The school also organized workshops for younger children to sensitize them about the need to refrain from interacting

---

[7] From an interview with Kishan Kejriwal in Kolkata on 16 February.

with strangers and discouraged them from leaving school with anyone apart from their parents. Discussions about topics of general awareness have now become a regular feature of their schedules, and all students attend a one-hour-long session once a week. Students who are unable to speak in front of the entire class are encouraged to speak to one of the three counsellors available.

Despite implementing such measures, Kishan voiced his concern about the vulnerability of students in any environment and the difficulties of running a school in the current times. 'Today, no place is really secure in that sense. In Yash's case, the accused person was known to the family and was aware of his school timings, and he went happily with him. If he had cried or raised an alarm, other students and the guard at every gate would have noticed,' he said.

Elaborating on the challenges they face on a day-to-day basis, Kishan gave the example of the escort-card system. The management has encountered several cases where parents of students made copies of their child's identity card so that more than one person could pick up the child from school. 'Parents have made colour photocopies of their escort card, which are laminated. In one case, the student's paternal and maternal grandmothers both had copies of the card. How are we supposed to ensure their safety if the family members don't comply with the rules?' said Kishan.

The year Yash died, the school management announced a scholarship of Rs 5000 in his memory for students who performed well in class. The money is contributed by the teachers of the school. In some cases, parents of the student donate it back to the school so that it can be given to a student from a less privileged background.

After Santosh's acquittal, Arabinda Naskar, the advocate who represented the prosecution, wrote to the state government in early 2015 urging it to appeal against the judgment at a higher court. Among the points he raised to counter the judgment, Arabinda highlighted the fact that the defence lawyers had not been able to prove that Santosh had indeed gone to his native place in Bihar at the time of the incident. Senior officials in the CID, however, said that there had been no word from the state government about appealing against the judgment. Four years have passed since then, and the chances of an appeal are not high.

While Anil has often considered taking the case forward in the high court, each time his family members have discouraged him from doing so. A year after Yash's death, Anil and his wife, Anita, had another child, a girl whom they named Palak. Besides Palak, they have another daughter, who was older than Yash. 'Since the incident took place, the women in our family are scared that something else may happen to the other children in the family. For their sake, we decided not to pursue the case in a higher court,' he said. But he is unable to fathom how the state government has managed to remain silent on the issue and has not appealed in the high court yet. Both the family of the victim and the state (police) have a right to appeal against a judgment given by a lower court at any point of time. Usually, the state appeals in cases where the judgment is not as expected. In case both appeal, then the cases are clubbed together.

After Yash's body was found in January 2009, the *Telegraph* reported that residents of Howrah put up roadblocks at several points on G.T. Road, Netaji Subhas Road and Panchanantala Road as a sign of protest, demanding the arrest of the culprits.[8] Mamata Banerjee, the current chief minister of West Bengal, who was then the opposition leader from Trinamool Congress, rushed to Howrah to stand by the Lakhotia family.

Thoroughly disappointed with the outcome of the case, Nandkishore believes that the political developments in the state may have been the reason for the laid-back attitude of the current state government. He pointed out that the government had changed since the incident. 'Since our family was well known in the area, political leaders had also got involved. The issue had become a reason for conflict between political parties,' he said. Nandkishore added that after the change in government, the investigation of the case slowed down significantly and the appeal of the judgment has been pending till date.

Expressing his frustration with the legal system, Anil said that the court might feel that the case has reached its conclusion even though no one has been held accountable for the murder of his son. 'We were never able to understand how the court could free Santosh. We lost Yash, and neither the police nor the CID has really tried to find the people who killed my son. Even if we believe that Santosh had nothing to do with it, we have to live each day knowing that the real culprits are still out there,' he said.

For the past nine years, the Lakhotias have been conducting a blood donation camp in Yash's memory for the general public. But for Anil and Anita, none of it has been able to take away the pain, anger and helplessness they

---

[8] https://www.telegraphindia.com/states/west-bengal/revenge-whiff-in-boy-kidnap/cid/1261223

continue to feel even today while looking at the pictures of a happy-go-lucky Yash. Apart from losing their child, they have also lost all faith in the system that failed to punish those responsible for the brutal murder of their innocent son.

* * *

Unlike the other nine cases in this book, Yash Lakhotia's is the only one that is unsolved till date, since the only accused person who was arrested was later acquitted of all charges. The investigation didn't progress any further beyond Santosh's acquittal.

Since the case is nearly a decade old, it was challenging to find all the pieces of the story. Even after I did manage to track down the people I would need to interview to get an objective understanding of what happened, there were times when I heard contradictory perspectives while interviewing different people. To avoid any confusion, I had to rely heavily on the documents to paint an accurate picture, which included official statements of the witnesses submitted in court.

Based on the facts presented by Yash's father as well as the CID officials, the police failed to collect the relevant evidence in the proper manner. As a result, no one was ever held accountable for kidnapping and killing Yash.

Nearly a decade after the unfortunate death of the seven-year-old boy, the family still hasn't got any closure. They don't know the reason behind his kidnapping or how he was killed. While they are convinced that Santosh was responsible, they continue to hope that the state government will either appeal against the order or find the real culprit.

8

Adit Ranka, Mumbai

For more than two decades, Nemichand and Shashi Ranka and their son, Himanshu, lived with Nemichand's brother, Jitendra, his wife, Chandrika, and their two children, Adit and Nishit, at 9th Lane, Khetwadi, a residential neighbourhood on Grant Road, Mumbai. It was only after Himanshu got married in 2011 that he moved to a new house, a couple of buildings away but still on the same lane with his wife and parents. Even though Himanshu was thirty and Adit only thirteen, the cousins were like brothers.

The move didn't change Adit and Himanshu's relationship much. In fact, Adit would often spend the night at Himanshu's house.

The Rankas were a close-knit Marwari family, and Chandrika's late husband, Jitendra, who passed away in 2014, was close to his brother, Nemichand, the eldest in the family. Himanshu was the son of Nemichand's younger sister, and everyone in the family knew that they had adopted him when he was just two years old. But this never got in the way of the close bond between Himanshu, Adit and Nishit while they were growing up.

The year was 2013, and 13 May fell on a Monday. Adit had spent the previous night at Himanshu's house as he often did during the summer vacations. He returned home around 10 a.m. His cousin brother had returned from Rajasthan at 6.30 a.m. the same day

Adit's father, Jitendra, worked as a diamond merchant. On that particular day, he left home around 11 a.m. to attend an event in Bandra Kurla Complex (BKC), with his elder son, Nishit. Chandrika, Adit's mother, recalled that her son's cousins, who lived in Surat, were visiting at the time.[1] When Adit came home, he sat down to watch television with them.

A personable child, Adit, known as 'Chikki' to his friends, family and neighbours, loved spending time with his family, especially his cousins. Being the youngest in the family, everyone doted on him. While Chandrika was busy in the kitchen, the landline rang around 12.15 p.m. Adit picked up the phone. When his mother came out of the kitchen, Adit told her that the call was from Jitendra's friend who had asked him to come to the 10th Lane in Khetwadi and collect the keys Jitendra had left with him.

The caller, however, hadn't mentioned which keys were meant to be picked up. Since her husband and her son had gone to attend the event in BKC, Chandrika assumed that they had left in someone else's car and sent their car keys back home. Chandrika asked Adit to go and collect the keys. Adit, however, went back to watching television with his cousins

---

[1] From an interview with Chandrika Ranka in Mumbai on 3 March 2018.

and forgot all about the phone call. Chandrika kept reminding her son to get dressed, and only after she had chased him around the house did he go to bathe.

While Adit was in the bathroom, the landline phone, which didn't have a caller ID at the time, rang once again. It was 12.30 p.m. and this time, Chandrika answered the call. 'The person who called said, "You didn't come?". When I asked who he was, he said, "*Adit aaya nahi* (Adit never showed up)". When I told him he was just leaving, he said, "Okay", and disconnected the call,' said Chandrika.

She asked Adit why he hadn't gone to collect the keys, considering the man had been waiting for a long time. Adit simply ignored his mother once again and changed the subject. Adit was reluctant to go since he wanted to play with his cousins. 'Chikki threw a tantrum about it. He was angry because he wanted to go to Himanshu's house with his cousins. He thought that if he went to get the keys, they would leave him behind,' said Chandrika. She gave up and went back to the kitchen.

* * *

When she came out into the living room around 12.45 p.m., all three of them had left the house. She looked down from her window and spotted Adit trying to convince his cousin Anisha to go along with him. Chandrika thought that it was silly of Adit to force his cousin to accompany him when he had to simply go to the next street. It would take him only a few minutes. Just as she was about to ask Adit to leave his cousin alone, she saw him take off on his own.

She watched Adit disappear around the corner and went back to her daily chores. She assumed that he would collect the keys and go straight to Himanshu's house to spend time with his cousins. In the next few minutes, the landline phone rang for the third time at 1 p.m. When Chandrika answered the phone, the caller asked for her husband's mobile number. 'This caller's voice was very different from the one who had called the first time. When I inquired about who he was, he identified himself as Rajesh. I gave him the number but later it struck me as odd that someone who had his landline number did not have his mobile number,' said Chandrika.

A couple of minutes later, Adit's father, Jitendra, received a call on his mobile number at 1.02 p.m., while he was still in BKC. The caller said '*Apka ladka Adit hamare paas hai. Agar ladka vapas chahiye to hame 30 peti de do* (Your son Adit is with us. If you want your son back, then give us Rs 30 lakh)'. While trying to wrap his head around what he had just heard, Jitendra asked who was calling. The caller yet again identified himself as Rajesh. Dismissing it as a prank call, Jitendra hung up.

Something didn't feel right to Jitendra. He decided to check with his family. The first person he called was his elder brother, Nemichand, to ask about his son's whereabouts. A couple of phone calls later, he realized that his son had indeed been kidnapped.

Meanwhile, an unsuspecting Chandrika was busy tending to her housework when she received a call from Nemichand who asked if Adit was home. Chandrika, who assumed all along that Adit was at his uncle's house, was left stunned when Nemichand broke the news to her that her son had been kidnapped for ransom.

* * *

A conversation with her husband cleared it all up. They realized that the keys had been a ruse to get Adit out of the house. Jitendra clarified that he had not sent any keys back home. Amid feelings of confusion, denial and fear, Chandrika's mind raced over the past one hour, and all the pieces of the puzzle came together—the phone calls asking Adit to come get the keys, another one asking for her husband's mobile number. Jitendra knew what had to be done. He immediately set out for the V.P. Road police station to report the kidnapping of his son.

Chandrika was unwilling to accept the fact that her son had been abducted. She ran out of the house to look for him, inquiring if the neighbours had seen him. 'I was barely in my senses and ran out of my building without any slippers. Everyone in the neighbourhood knew him. So, I went to the 10th Lane and asked all the shopkeepers around if they had seen him,' she said.

* * *

Additional Commissioner of Police Krishna Prakash, who has dealt with many incidents of kidnapping in the past, was in charge of the case. Speaking from experience, he said that the best way to deal with ransom calls was to prolong them for as long as possible.[2]

In cases where the victim recognizes the kidnapper, 99 per cent of the times, the kidnapper will end up killing the victim out of fear of being caught. 'Parents should inform the

---

[2] From an interview with Krishna Prakash in Mumbai on 3 March 2018.

police in a discreet manner, like directly getting in touch with
the senior police inspector of the area instead of being seen
walking into a police station. One shouldn't take the chance
of being seen speaking to the police as it may put the child's
life at risk,' said Krishna. He added that if the kidnapper had
committed the crime for a ransom, he would ideally prefer to
keep the child alive until he gets the money, unless there is an
intention to kill the victim.

Once the complaint was registered, Inspector Shrikant
Desai, who was the investigating officer, said that since the
ransom call had already been made, the case would have to
be treated as one of kidnapping and not as a missing-person's
case.[3] The police tracked the phone number the ransom
call was made from and found that it belonged to a public
telephone booth in Sion. The trail went cold from there, and
they were unable to find another clue.

* * *

As the police investigation would later go on to reveal, at this
point, Adit wasn't with any stranger. He had left with twenty-
eight-year-old Vijesh Sanghvi, a close friend of Himanshu's,
in a white Honda City car that Vijesh had borrowed from his
friend, Shailesh Bokadia. Vijesh and Himanshu both worked
in the metal market and spent a lot of time together. He was
familiar to Adit, as they had met on various occasions before.
After Vijesh drove out of Khetwadi, he went to the Vodafone
Gallery in Sion to get his Nano SIM card changed. There,

---

[3] From an interview with Shrikant Desai in Mumbai on 14
October 2017.

he submitted his driving licence as identity proof. He then made the ransom call from a public telephone booth nearby. In the CCTV footage of the Vodafone Gallery in Sion, which was later presented as evidence in the case, Adit is seen with Vijesh. 'While Vijesh went out to make the ransom call, he gave Adit his mobile phone to play games on to keep him occupied. Both of them can be seen clearly in the CCTV footage,' said Shrikant.

Shortly after they entered, Vijesh was seen leaving the gallery at 12.57 p.m. and re-entering at 1.05 p.m. According to the police, Vijesh left with Adit after making the ransom call and drove to Chembur as per the original plan he had hatched with his alleged accomplice, none other than Adit's cousin—Himanshu Ranka. While he was on his way, he received a call from Himanshu at 1.11 p.m. As per the call data records, the conversation lasted 104 seconds. The police suspected that during this call, Himanshu informed Vijesh that Adit's father had approached the police.

Explaining his observations, Shrikant said, 'Since the Ranka family belonged to the Marwari community, Himanshu had expected Jitendra to come to him first, since he knew that people of the community didn't like to deal with the police much. But things didn't go as planned since Jitendra went to the police instead, after which Himanshu asked Vijesh not to bring Adit back home.'

After speaking to Himanshu, Vijesh continued to drive and crossed the Kharpada Toll Naka before continuing on towards Pali, in Raigad district. Shrikant added that since Vijesh had a factory in Pali, he knew the area and the roads well. After he got there, he went to a public phone booth and borrowed the booth owner Kalpesh Jadhav's mobile phone.

Referring to Kalpesh's statement, the police said Vijesh walked away from the shop and called Himanshu. This phone call lasted for 105 seconds, and Vijesh and Himanshu had an argument. 'Himanshu told him that things hadn't gone as planned, and that police officials from the crime branch and other departments had reached their house. In the end, Himanshu told him, *'Tu tera dekh le, main apna dekh lunga* (You figure things out for yourself, I'll do the same),' said Shrikant.

After the FIR was registered around 2.30 p.m., around twenty to twenty-five police personnel visited the 10th Lane at Khetwadi where the boy had been just before he went missing. As soon as the media heard about the case, senior police officials got involved, and policemen from several departments joined in to look for clues. While the police were trying to collect details about the people the family was close to, Vijesh reached the Ranka residence around 9.30 p.m.

Considering Adit's love for cricket, the police decided to look for him at Wankhede Stadium where a cricket match was under way that day. Jitendra and other family members set out to accompany the police in their search as well as to meet the additional commissioner of police, Krishna, who was at the stadium. In his attempt to blend in, Vijesh joined the search, and volunteered to drive them to Wankhede Stadium.

This is when Adit's family members chanced upon a crucial piece of evidence. According to Chandrika and her brother, Surendra Jain, when Jitendra was seated in the front seat of the car Vijesh was driving, he spotted a pair of red-and-blue Crocs by his feet on the floor of the car. These shoes resembled the ones he had recently bought for Adit.

He remembered them particularly because Adit had thrown a tantrum to buy them during their family holiday in Dubai just a week before the incident.

Eventually, it would be these red-and-blue Crocs that would lead to the arrest of Vijesh and later Himanshu. However, the sequence of events that led to the arrest is remembered differently by the police and the family members of the victim.

After finding the shoes, Jitendra voiced his suspicions to Himanshu, who apparently was quick to dismiss them. 'When my husband told him that the shoes could be Adit's, Himanshu flatly said that it wasn't possible and that the shoes probably belonged to Shailesh's children, the man whose car Vijesh had borrowed. Had he been truly worried about finding Adit, he would have at least confronted Vijesh about it instead of casually dismissing it, especially since he was not around all day, Chandrika said.

Recalling the events of that night, Surendra said that Vijesh's and Himanshu's behaviour had seemed suspicious to him as well as other members of Adit's family in more than one way. Surendra recalled that while they were waiting at Adit's house for some news from the police, Himanshu had brought up the topic of the ransom demand. 'He insisted that we should give Rs 30 lakh to the kidnapper. I told him that we would have paid Rs 50 lakh if only we knew whom to pay the money to, since the kidnapper had not called back. While we were all trying to think of where Adit could be, Himanshu was only thinking about the ransom,' he said.

Thinking back, Shrikant recalled that Vijesh yelled at the police for not being able to find Adit when he joined the search. Chandrika also remembered that during a conversation with her brother-in-law, Nemichand, Vijesh had told him that whoever kidnapped Adit must be someone within the family.

Surendra said that after Jitendra told him about the footwear, they decided to keep it to themselves and come up with a ruse to convince Vijesh to drive the car to the V.P. Road police station. Their hopes of finding Adit grew.

When Vijesh was out of earshot, Surendra informed the police about the slippers. On their way back from Wankhede Stadium, Jitendra told Vijesh that he wanted to give some additional information to the police and asked him to take them to V.P. Road police station before going home.

Completely unaware of their intentions, Vijesh readily agreed to drive them there. Once they reached the police station, Surendra saw that the police were already waiting for them. But in order to be absolutely sure, the police needed Chandrika to confirm that the shoes indeed belonged to Adit. They asked Jitendra to discreetly bring his wife there. Jitendra called her and asked her to get ready and left to go pick her up.

When Chandrika reached the police station around 11 p.m., she remembered seeing Vijesh and Himanshu standing together near the steps while the police were waiting near the car. Chandrika recognized the shoes immediately. She was, however, confused when she saw the police take Himanshu along with Vijesh into their custody the moment she confirmed that the shoes belonged to Adit. The police ushered Jitendra and his family members into one of the rooms and asked them to wait there. They took Vijesh and Himanshu into different rooms and questioned them separately.

Shrikant said that while they were tracking the landline number that Jitendra had received the ransom call from, the police were also simultaneously tracking the location of several people who were close to the family. Analysis of the call data records revealed that Vijesh's location was close to the phone booth in Sion at the time the ransom call was made.

While the Ranka family struggled to figure out how Himanshu could be involved in Adit's kidnapping, a few policemen came into the room and assured them that since they had found Adit's slippers, it wouldn't be long before they found him as well. They then advised them to go home and wait.

Chandrika remembered the feeling of calm washing over her. She believed that Himanshu's friend had taken Adit and must have kept him somewhere. It was only a matter of time before he would come home, she told herself.

Once Vijesh was arrested and brought to the police station, Shrikant said that their immediate concern was to rescue the boy as soon as possible. In the initial stage of the interrogation, the police assumed that Adit was still alive. They tried to rush their efforts to find him.

* * *

The police examined the car. Apart from the slippers, they also noticed some bloodstains near the trunk. During his interrogation, Shrikant said that Vijesh confessed to having kidnapped Adit and agreed to take them to the spot where he had assaulted him. It wasn't long before the rest of the story came out.

The police believe that the last call made between Vijesh and Himanshu sealed Adit's fate. It was then that Vijesh decided to kill Adit, since taking him back home would have surely implicated him. Having made up his mind, he got into the car and continued to drive for another 100 metres before he stopped in front of a grocery shop. Here, he purchased a kitchen knife, one cigarette, a matchbox and a packet of chips. Since the shopkeeper, Prashant Mehta, didn't keep cigarettes in his shop, he sent his errand boy to fetch it from another shop. Mehta, who later appeared as one of the witnesses, said that he had seen Vijesh come in a white car with a boy ten to twelve years old seated in the front seat.

Having found all the things he needed, Vijesh then set out to scout for places where he could kill Adit without attracting attention. He stopped the car at an isolated spot near the Amba River in Sudhagad Taluka around 6 p.m. As soon as Adit stepped out of the car, Vijesh attacked him with the knife. Based on his confession, the police said that Vijesh slit Adit's wrists and stabbed him multiple times in the chest, neck and stomach. He assaulted him so hard that the kitchen knife broke during the tussle. He, however, didn't succeed in killing the boy, who begged him over and over to stop. He cried out for help as he continued to bleed profusely.

In a desperate attempt to silence him once and for all, Vijesh collected some dry grass and lit a fire. He grabbed Adit and threw him on the burning grass. Even though the flames were not big enough to completely engulf him, Adit suffered substantial burns on his face and other parts of his body. Vijesh then tossed his body into the trunk of the car while he tried to figure out the best way to dispose of the body.

From Amba River, he drove for another 25 kilometres towards Pune and around 7 p.m., dumped the body along with the broken knife in the bushes near the Mumbai–Pune Expressway in Panvel. Shrikant said it was possible that Adit was alive when he was thrown into the trunk of the car. He possibly died by the time he was dumped in the bushes out of sight of passing vehicles. Vijesh then drove back to Khetwadi and crossed the Vashi Toll Naka around 8.45 p.m.

Around 4.30 p.m. on 14 May, he led the police to the spot near Amba River where he had stabbed Adit and tried to burn him. After they examined the spot, the police corroborated that Adit had been killed in the cruel manner that Vijesh had described.

Shrikant added that Vijesh initially denied killing Adit and tried to misguide the police when they asked him to take them to the spot where he had dumped the body. But finally, he conceded, and around 6 p.m., led them to the bushes where he had thrown the body.

When the police found the body, Adit's face was partially burnt and his intestines were bulging out. His body was identified by his elder brother, Nishit, who recognized the white watch on his hand that he had recently purchased in Dubai. Since Adit's face had burn injuries, the police called for a DNA test, which confirmed his identity. The body was then sent to J.J. Hospital for a post-mortem.

The post-mortem report stated that Adit had died of unnatural causes, which included multiple injuries and burns. The report also noted that Adit had suffered head injuries in the form of skull fractures and haemorrhage along with stab wounds all over his body. After spending the entire day hoping to see her son walk in through the front door, Chandrika finally heard about her son's death after the body was identified at night on 14 May.

Though the manner in which Adit was killed was gruesome, the reason behind committing the crime was a common one—the need for money. Shrikant said that both

Vijesh and Himanshu had suffered substantial losses in betting over cricket matches and had debts to repay to several people.

The police claimed that they found several witnesses who said that Vijesh had lost Rs 7 lakh earlier that month while Himanshu had lost around Rs 95,000. They had both promised to pay up soon. While the witnesses the police had gathered confirmed that Vijesh was indeed involved in cricket betting and had pending debts, they, however, denied knowing Himanshu.

At the centre of the kidnapping and murder case was a sum of Rs 30 lakh that Jitendra had collected on behalf of his friend, Anil Jain, on 10 May and kept at his house as a favour to him since Anil was unable to pick it up. Shrikant said that Himanshu had known about the money in the house, and he, along with Vijesh, decided to kidnap Adit in exchange for a ransom, with which they had planned to pay off the debts they had incurred.

* * *

On 9 October 2017, an invisible line ran down the middle of courtroom number nineteen of the Mumbai City Civil and Sessions Court, separating the defence from the prosecution. The members of the Ranka family that had lived happily in the same house for twenty long years stood in the same courtroom but on opposite ends. As the judge, S.B. Agrawal, entered the courtroom, representatives of both sides waited anxiously for him to speak and so did the two men, Vijesh Sanghvi and Himanshu Ranka, who had been accused in the kidnapping and murder of thirteen-year-old Adit Ranka.

A lot happened over the next two minutes. As soon as the judge sat down, in a clear voice, he said that accused number one had been convicted and accused number two had been acquitted. While Adit's mother, Chandrika, and her friends were still trying to make sense of what had happened, Himanshu sank to his knees and burst out crying. Vijesh had an expression of utter shock on his face.

Clarity came in a few seconds when Himanshu started thanking the judge over and over as he wept into his hands. As per the order given by the sessions court,[4] Vijesh was sentenced to life imprisonment, while Himanshu was given the benefit of the doubt and acquitted of all charges. As the latter's family members rejoiced in one corner of the courtroom, there was crestfallen silence on the other side, where Chandrika stood in stoic silence.

Contrary to the version remembered by Chandrika in which her late husband had found the slippers, the police, in the charge sheet, stated that they had found the slippers on 15 May after they seized the car from Vijesh's house, which were then identified by the victim's mother.

The discrepancy between the two versions was addressed during the trial in court and the police maintained that they had not arrested or detained either Vijesh or Himanshu on 13 May since they didn't have any cogent evidence against them. In his statement, while Shrikant admitted that both of them had come to the police station around 11 p.m. on the night Adit was kidnapped, he did not interrogate them at the time

---

4 *The State vs Vijesh Pawanraj Sanghvi & Himanshu Nemichand Ranka*, Sessions Case No. 761 of 2013 (Bombay City Civil and Sessions Court, 4 January 2016).

or detain them. Leaving things open-ended, he added that he was unable to say whether any other officer had interrogated them.

The evidence that the police had found incriminated Vijesh. Based on the charge sheet, they arrested him around 1 p.m. on 14 May from his residence which was close to the Ranka home. Himanshu was also arrested on the same day. Based on the details mentioned in the judgment, while arresting him, the police seized two mobile phones from Vijesh and also noted that there were 'burn marks near his right wrist'.

On 13 May, ten phone calls were made between Vijesh and Himanshu between 10.32 a.m. and 10.52 p.m., and according to the police, the calls were the basis of a 'theory of conspiracy' between the two. While Himanshu made only two of those phone calls, Vijesh made the rest, one from Kalpesh's mobile phone in Pali and others from his own. Referring to them as scanty evidence, the judge observed that there were no details of the conversation that took place between the two, and the calls couldn't be treated as substantive evidence by themselves.

Apart from the testimonies of the witnesses, the police also collected a lot of evidence that seemed to corroborate Vijesh's confession of the brutal manner in which Adit was killed. The knife, for instance, was recovered in two parts. While the white hilt was recovered on 14 May, Vijesh reportedly showed the police where he had thrown the 14-cm-long bloodstained blade, which was found on 17 May at the base of a peepul tree near the spot where he attacked Adit.

The police also collected pieces of burnt clothes and hair. A day after Vijesh was arrested, the police recovered his yellow shirt and a pair of black trousers from his house. Both had bloodstains on them. Predictably, an analysis of the samples indicated that the blood belonged to Adit.

The police also collected electronic evidence that clearly indicated that Adit had been with Vijesh after he went missing from his house. Apart from the CCTV footage collected from the Vodafone Gallery in Sion and the call data records, Adit and Vijesh were seen together in the car at the Kharpada Toll Naka. The CCTV footage at Vashi Toll Naka, however, showed that Vijesh was alone on his way back to Khetwadi.

* * *

After the initial outrage surrounding Adit's kidnapping died down, Chandrika's struggle during the four-and-a-half-year-long legal tussle was a lonely one, as she lost much more than her son along the way. Adit's sudden death deeply affected his family members. While they tried to piece their life back together, Jitendra, who was suffering from a fatal lung disease, passed away about ten months after the incident.

Choking back tears, Chandrika said that Jitendra was shattered after the incident. Due to stress, he never quite recovered, and his condition continued to deteriorate until he died of heart failure. 'He stopped speaking to anyone. He was completely broken and continued to suffer internally. Even after he started going to work, people would tell me that he would go to the diamond market, sit and cry for some time and then come back home,' she said.

It was due to the undying support of her son and the parents of Adit's classmates that Chandrika was able to find the strength to attend the hearings till the end. But considering that she had to face her family on the other side of the courtroom, the journey was not an easy one for her.

Her statement against Himanshu did not go down well with her brother-in-law, Nemichand, and his other family members. As the case progressed, Nemichand's family further distanced themselves from her, and they would go to the sessions court separately for the hearings.

Without the support of her family, she found herself isolated, even though she tried her level best to maintain a relationship with Himanshu's family. 'Over the course of the trial, our relationship soured. In the early days, he was apologetic about Himanshu's involvement but later his attitude changed. Every time Himanshu's bail plea was rejected, they would come home and fight with us. In the past, they tried to pressurize me and my husband to support Himanshu. But we knew that we would have to fight to get justice for our son,' she said.

Chandrika recalled how hard it was to watch her entire family support Himanshu while she sat alone at the other end of the courtroom, despite being a part of the Ranka family for twenty-six long years. Sitting through hearings where the evidence related to Adit's murder was shown was emotionally taxing for Chandrika and her son, Nishit, who was only twenty years old when the trial began. The worst of such hearings was on the day the knife used to stab Adit was produced in court.

Recounting the day, Chandrika said that when the knife was presented, it was bent and in two pieces. 'Nishit was horrified to see the condition of the knife as he then realized how much his brother had suffered before his death. He was so upset that he ran out of the courtroom. I followed him, and by the time I caught up with him, he had already left the building and was banging the iron gate of the court so loudly that a couple of policemen came and threatened to arrest him,' she said. Thankfully, the policemen empathized with her once she explained the situation to them.

She, however, failed to calm Nishit down. He kept saying, '*Knife mud gaya? Knife kaise mud gaya? Kaise maara usko?* (The knife got bent? How did the knife bend? How did he kill him?)' over and over. Considering his disturbed state of mind, Chandrika could not think of letting him go alone, and even though all her belongings were in the courtroom, she decided to leave with him.

After Himanshu's acquittal, the relationship between the two sides of the family has gradually improved with time. Chandrika now has a cordial relationship with Himanshu's wife, Jinal, and his parents. Despite repeated attempts made by Himanshu and his family members, Chandrika has firmly refused to meet him or make amends with him. She admits that after he came back to his home, she had a tough time staying in her house, knowing that the person who may have contributed to the death of her son continued to live just down the lane.

Even though Himanshu has been acquitted of all the charges that were levelled against him, Chandrika is unable to accept that he had nothing to do with Adit's kidnapping. 'The disappointment of all the parents who supported us for Himanshu's acquittal was more than their happiness for the life sentence given to Vijesh. It felt as though my son got only half the justice he deserved,' she said.

Since the case involves her close relatives, Chandrika didn't wish to appeal against the verdict. But she did pin her hopes on the state government who she thought would appeal against the order given by the sessions court. Neither the police nor the prosecution, however, felt the same. The special public prosecutor, Kalpana Chavan, felt that the evidence presented against Himanshu was too weak.[5] Since the phone calls, which were the only evidence linking the two accused, were explained by Himanshu's advocate during the trial, an appeal in the Bombay High Court was unlikely to stand. Apart from the inadequate evidence, Jitendra, who had been a crucial witness, passed away before the trial could begin. This left many questions unanswered.

Throughout the trial, Kalpana felt that there were several loopholes in the police investigation, which benefited the defence lawyers and were exploited by them to build their argument, including the disputed claim made by the police that the slippers and the car were recovered on 15 May instead of 13 May, the day of the incident. Blaming the police for the poor collection of evidence, Kalpana said, 'Perhaps the investigating officers were not intelligent enough, but there were too many lacunae in the investigation. Due to their inadvertence, incompetence or overconfidence, we were not able to make the connection between Vijesh and Himanshu.'

She further pointed out that due to the carelessness of the police, they were not able to check if Vijesh and Himanshu had exchanged messages with each other or had a voice-altering application on their phones. She explained that at the time their mobile phones were taken into custody, the police

---

[5] From an interview with Kalpana Chavan in Mumbai on 8 March 2018.

had made them unlock their phones and checked their call records. However, the police did not note down the passcodes required to unlock the phones, and both of them refused to share them when they were asked again later. The Forensic Science Laboratory couldn't analyse the contents of their phones since they were unable to open the devices.

Apart from insufficient evidence, Kalpana said that all the important witnesses against Himanshu either turned hostile or never appeared before the court. 'The bookies later denied knowing Himanshu, and the *paanwala*, who had seen Vijesh and Himanshu talking around 10.30 a.m. on the day Adit was kidnapped, never appeared in court. Even though the police recorded his statement, they didn't keep a watch on him and he disappeared,' said Kalpana.

Even though Himanshu's advocate has denied the allegations in court, Kalpana still maintains that either directly or indirectly, Himanshu knew about the Rs 30 lakh that was kept in the house. She pointed out that based on what Jitendra had told the police and as seen in the call data records, there was one phone conversation with Himanshu in which Jitendra casually told him about the Rs 30 lakh he had kept in his house since they were close family members. This part, however, was not highlighted in the charge sheet by the police.

Defending the police's stand, Shrikant insisted that Himanshu was acquitted because he tampered with the evidence and witnesses. He added that during the trial, Vijesh and Himanshu would try various tactics to lead the witnesses astray. 'They dressed up in identical clothes, white shirt and blue jeans for five or six hearings to confuse the witnesses, possibly on the advice of their lawyer,' he said.

Even though the police stated that Vijesh had confessed to kidnapping and subsequently killing Adit during the trial, he denied being involved in any of it. Pleading his innocence, Vijesh's advocate, B.P. Singh, argued that when Vijesh had gone to Vodafone Gallery in Sion to exchange his SIM card, he had apparently seen Himanshu's friend DJ who was with Adit.

Vijesh insisted that when he entered the Vodafone Gallery, Adit followed him. However, Kalpana pointed out that Vijesh never mentioned anything about this person to the police at the time of his interrogation. He was also unable to provide any information about Adit's whereabouts after the visit to the Vodafone Gallery, and the judge treated his statement as a false and imaginary story. Vijesh's advocates have now appealed against the life sentence in the Bombay High Court.

For his co-accused, Himanshu, who earned his freedom the hard way, the four-and-a-half-year-long trial was a harrowing time for him and his family. Till date, the police believe that Vijesh couldn't have planned the kidnapping without the help of an inside man like Himanshu.

* * *

Vijesh was one of Himanshu's best friends, and they had known each other since class VIII. The news of Vijesh's involvement in the murder of his brother came as a rude shock to Himanshu. On the first day that they were placed together in prison, Himanshu said that he was enraged at Vijesh for having killed his brother and ruining his life over some money. He punched Vijesh, after which they were placed in separate barracks.

Though the advocates who represented Himanshu in court worked hard to get him acquitted, he feels that he owes it all to his wife, Jinal, who stood by him throughout the trial and closely studied all the evidence to help the advocates prove his innocence.[6]

Himanshu blamed the police for fabricating details in the charge sheet and framing him without any evidence at all, which landed him in jail for more than four years. 'I didn't have a financial crunch back then nor am I going through one now. But the police simply wanted to show that they had solved the case in a day, and to make it a sensational case, they came up with the story of a cousin who planned the kidnapping of his brother. They should realize that by falsifying facts, an innocent can also be charged,' said Himanshu.

Himanshu said that while they were in police custody, he had asked Vijesh why he had mentioned his name to the police and was surprised when Vijesh denied doing so. Vijesh told him that the police had forced him to give Himanshu's name.

Himanshu added that the police treated him unfairly while he was in their custody. Apart from beating him up, they did not readily allow him to meet his advocate. Even when they did, he was able to speak for only a few minutes.

Even though he is glad to be back home with his family, Himanshu continues to be bitter about the manner in which the media covered the facts of the case. He felt that the newspapers and television channels were heavily biased against him and never considered that he might be

6   From an interview with Himanshu Ranka in Mumbai on 18 March 2018.

innocent. He felt that it was unfair that even though Vijesh kidnapped and murdered his brother, the media placed the entire blame on him without giving him a chance to speak up in his defence.

His legal troubles aside, Himanshu lost a brother whom he was extremely fond of. He insisted that it was impossible for him to even think about harming Adit in any way. 'If I would have gone to jail for any other reason, I would have been fine with it. But being accused of killing my own brother left me devastated. Adit was very attached to me, and he would spend more time at our house than in his own,' said Himanshu. He added that apart from the four and a half years of his life that he lost, his father lost his reputation and he his career.

Himanshu and Jinal say they want to forget everything that has happened and focus on their future together. Apart from rebuilding their lives, Himanshu hopes to fix his relationship with Chandrika some day, regardless of how much time it might take.

Despite all the cold vibes between them, Himanshu holds no grudge against his aunt and doesn't want to look back. Unwilling to waste any more time on the past, Himanshu said, 'I wasted nearly five years in jail and lost everything during that time. I'm now trying to rebuild my life slowly, and I am not interested in finding the truth since our only goal is to go ahead in life.'

Vijesh's actions, which led to the death of an innocent thirteen-year-old boy and the four-and-a-half-year-long legal battle, caused an insurmountable rift among the members of the Ranka family. They didn't just lose a family member, but trust and faith among themselves. Even after Himanshu returned home and they started speaking to each other, both sides knew that things would never be quite the same again.

* * *

In tough times, the support of one's family is something most people rely on. In Chandrika's case, however, her fight to get justice for her son pitted her against other members of her rather close-knit family. Despite losing her husband shortly after her son's murder, Chandrika battled through the long trial alone, leaning largely on her son and the parents of Adit's classmates for support.

On most days, she would travel from her home to the sessions court alone and with each hearing, her confidence grew. She steeled herself on days the details of the brutal murder would be discussed at length. She gradually acquainted herself with the process of a criminal trial and later told me that she would often come up with suggestions that could possibly strengthen the prosecution's case. On the last day, even though Kalpana, the prosecution advocate, expected this verdict, Chandrika refused to give up hope until the judgment was out.

Chandrika confided in me that there were days when she would contemplate moving out of her house, which is just a two-minute walk from Himanshu's. She eventually dismissed the idea, realizing that it would change nothing but geography.

From the beginning of the trial till this day, the strength and grace that she has displayed in maintaining a cordial relationship with Himanshu's family is admirable, to say the least. Sadly, it seems as though the damage caused by the investigation and the trial to their relationship is irreparable.

After the exhausting trial, Chandrika is now trying to move on. Apart from appearing on the display pictures of her social media profiles from time to time, Adit can be spotted on pretty much every wall of her home. Not a day goes by when Chandrika doesn't think of Adit. But now she tries to remember her jolly and loving son in the pleasant memories that would leave a smile on her face.

9

Om Kharat, Pune

Over the years, kidnappers have learnt from the mistakes of others before them who were caught. They are more careful while planning an abduction and study the methods police officers use to nab criminals. Crime shows and the Internet also provide ample content on the subject. Law enforcement officers continuously update their methods, but kidnappers are exceedingly meticulous in their approach.

In the case of the kidnapping of seven-year-old Om Kharat, nothing was done on an impulse. From carrying out dry runs and stealing a SIM card to making duplicate licence plate numbers copied from old online advertisements selling cars, the kidnappers charted out every detail of their plan well in advance.

It had been eight years since the Kharats moved into their house in the quiet, residential neighbourhood of Purnanagar in Pimpri-Chinchwad, Pune, which is usually known to have a low crime rate. Om Kharat was a student of class II at the Global International School. Like any other seven-year-old boy, he loved spending his free time playing with his friends in the open space just outside his house.

On 23 September 2017, a Saturday, Om didn't have to go to school but had to attend his tuition classes before he could go out and play. Always an obedient child, Om woke up at 7.30 a.m., got dressed early and sat down to watch his favourite cartoon show, *Doraemon*.

He could only watch TV for about ten to fifteen minutes as he had to leave soon for his tuition classes, which started at 8 a.m. His classes, which took place just a couple of buildings away, ended at 10 a.m. Once they were over, his mother, Yogita, brought him back home. She later gave him a bath and fed him his lunch. She had planned to take him along for her yoga class later that evening before attending a social function.

Around 4.20 p.m., Om was ready and all set to leave with his mother. As he waited for his mother to get dressed, he shouted out to her that he was stepping outside to play with his friends. It was a fairly routine request and his mother thought nothing of it at the time.

Yogita got dressed, and ten minutes later she stepped out of the front door. She was about to call out to Om when she spotted her neighbours huddled on the street with a worried look on their faces. Yogita walked over to them.

It took her several minutes to fully understand what had happened. A white car with two passengers had picked up her son and driven off with him.

The child's father, Sandeep Kharat, ran a business of electrical panels from an office five minutes away from his house. Sandeep, who had left for his office after lunch around 2 p.m., was in for a rude shock. He received a phone call from his panic-stricken wife informing him that their son had been abducted. The news left him in a daze. He rushed back home.

Sandeep is still visibly shaken when he recalls the incident. 'Within a few minutes, someone kidnapped our son in broad daylight. He was taken in front of his friends while he was playing with them,' he said.[1]

In the next hour, calls went out to relatives and family friends who rushed to the Kharat residence to offer their support. After trying to wrap their heads around the incident, they came to a unanimous decision—to report the incident to the police.

Meanwhile, the word about a child being kidnapped from in front of his home had started doing the rounds. The news soon reached Vijay Kumar Palsule, senior police inspector of Nigdi police station. 'I got the news from an acquaintance of mine who called to inform that a child has been kidnapped in Purnanagar, Chikhali. I asked him to stay put and told him that I would meet him there,' said Vijay.[2] As he was getting ready to leave, however, Sandeep reached Nigdi police station.

Sandeep parked his car in the parking lot of the police station and was seconds away from meeting Vijay when he received a call on his mobile phone at 4.40 p.m. On the other end of the line was a man who told him that he had abducted Om. Stunned, Sandeep listened on as the kidnapper explained why he had resorted to such aggressive measures.

The caller said he had been cheated by Sandeep due to which he had incurred financial losses in his business. 'I had no recollection of doing such a thing,' said Sandeep, and asked him who he was. 'But I didn't get an answer to the

---

[1] From an interview with Sandeep Kharat in Pune on 11 November 2017.

[2] From an interview with Vijay Palsule in Pune on 11 November 2017.

question. I pleaded with him to give us our son back and told
him that we would give him whatever he wanted in return.
He said he would get in touch with me in an hour and a half
and cut the call.' Sandeep frantically tried calling back on the
same number multiple times but in vain. The kidnapper had
switched off his mobile phone.

While standing in the parking lot, Sandeep took a
moment to process all that had transpired in the last couple
of minutes. He realized that he had a worrying decision to
make. The kidnapper had warned him that he would never
see his son again if he tried to contact the police. Fearful of
the consequences, Sandeep decided to leave out the part about
the ransom call while talking to the police.

As he walked into the police station, he bumped into Vijay
at the entrance. The conversation between Vijay and Sandeep
was a quick exchange of introductions and a confirmation that
his child had been kidnapped. After this, they immediately
got into the police van and left for Sandeep's residence.

Vijay recalled that in the initial hours of their
acquaintance, Sandeep seemed to be visibly shaken. Even
though the police tried to question Sandeep in the car on the
way to his house, he wasn't willing to say much about what
had happened. Unaware of the ransom call, Vijay assumed
that perhaps his reluctance to talk stemmed from being in a
state of shock.

At the Kharat residence, the police followed their usual
protocol of questioning the neighbours and looked around for
any clue that would help them find the whereabouts of the
seven-year-old boy. When the police started talking to the
family members, some of Sandeep's family and friends took
Vijay aside and hinted that something was amiss.

With the boy's interest at heart, they confided in him that Sandeep had received a phone call from the kidnapper earlier that day. Suddenly, Sandeep's behaviour started to make sense. Vijay tried to convince the worried father to share more details while reassuring him that they would handle the situation with caution.

With a little more coaxing, Vijay was able to earn his trust, and Sandeep told him everything the kidnapper had said. 'The boy's father mentioned that the caller spoke in Hindi, which was helpful for us,' said Vijay.

Sandeep later admitted to being hesitant about telling the police about the phone call but was glad Vijay talked him into it. 'At the time, all I could think of was what if they found out that I approached the police and hurt my child? But the police and my friends advised me to share all the information I had, and after I did so, the police began their investigation in a prompt manner,' Sandeep said.

Apart from the obvious concern over finding the child, the Kharats were worried that Om would miss his mother before long. 'Om is deeply attached to his mother and doesn't eat or sleep without her. On the day they took him, we were very worried about how he would survive without his mother and how the kidnappers would react if he started crying,' said Sandeep.

Overseeing the entire rescue operation was the then Pune Police Commissioner Rashmi Shukla. 'I was concerned, worried and tense when I heard about it. In the past, every time, the kidnapped child had been killed. Rarely are children retrieved hale and hearty,' she said.[3] The police took certain

---

[3] From an interview with Rashmi Shukla in Pune on 7 March 2018.

precautions to ensure that the kidnappers remained unaware of their involvement.

The rescue operations were planned and monitored from the Kerala Bhavan in Pimpri-Chinchwad to avoid raising suspicion since there was a chance that someone could be watching Sandeep's house. Shukla gave standing instructions to all the police officials involved in the case, including senior officers, that they should not wear their uniform or travel by police vehicles.

The police tried to find CCTV footage that could throw up some information about the kidnappers or the vehicle they were travelling in. But there weren't any cameras installed in the neighbourhood.

While questioning the witnesses, the police came across an elderly lady who said she had spotted two men picking up Om. Questions about the description of the car and its occupants or details of the number plate didn't yield a lot of information. The lady could only recall that the car was white in colour and that the kidnappers had covered most of their faces to avoid being identified. As a crowd gathered near the Kharat residence, details of the car passed around like Chinese whispers. Some said it was a Tata Indica, others said it was a Santro. The police realized that the information was unreliable.

Sandeep's parents, along with other relatives who lived in Ahmednagar, came to the Kharat residence to offer moral support. Meanwhile, outside the house, the crowd had grown in number and included several policemen in civil clothes. This raised a red flag for one of the kidnappers, believed to be twenty-one-year-old Akshay Jamdare.

The police later found out that Akshay had allegedly kept a watch on the house while his accomplice, twenty-year-old

Roshan Shinde stayed back with Om, who was being held in a white Indica Vista parked far away from the Kharats' home.

As the nervous family members waited for the kidnapper's next call, Sandeep's phone rang. He picked it up and was caught off guard when the kidnapper said, 'Why are there so many people outside your house? You've told the police?' Though Sandeep vehemently denied it, the kidnapper told him that his accomplice was nearby and keeping a watch on the house.

The kidnapper's comment took the police by surprise as well, and they realized that he was trying to scare Sandeep. The call got the police concerned. Vijay realized that if one of the kidnapper's accomplices was keeping an eye on them, the child's life was in danger. They had to act fast.

The police tried to trace the location of the kidnapper from the call records of the mobile number that was used to make the ransom calls. On the ground, more than 100 policemen were deputed, and teams were formed to search any locations the police came across while tracking the number.

The search for the mobile number's owner led the police to a rather confused Sanjay Chavan[4] who hadn't even realized that he was missing a SIM card from his dual-SIM phone. The police brought him in for questioning, which continued till 25 September. To ensure all possibilities were examined thoroughly, the police checked his call records to find out if he had any connection with the kidnappers and brought in the frequent callers on the list for questioning as well.

As the pieces of the puzzle came together, Senior Inspector Vijay realized that the kidnappers had stolen the SIM card to

---

[4] Name changed.

throw the police off their scent, and Sanjay had nothing to do with it. The police discovered that the kidnappers had stolen the SIM card from a mobile phone that had been kept on charge in a tyre repair shop on Dehu Moshi Road. They had traced the number and found Chavan's address, which was the tyre shop. Sanjay Chavan's phone had a damaged screen, and he never realized that one of his SIM cards had gone missing. Vijay added that the kidnappers were smart enough to know that the owner of the SIM card would be the obvious target of the police.

Time was running out, and the police were still not close to knowing who the real kidnappers were. Pune Police Commissioner Shukla referred to the initial phase of the investigation as tricky. Even after detailed questioning of the parents and neighbours, they had few suspects in mind and fewer concrete leads to follow.

In most cases, the police track the IMEI number of the handset to find a person's broad location. But since the kidnappers switched off their mobile phones immediately after making the call, the police were unable to track their movement.

While the police knew that Om had been kidnapped by a person known to the family, Shukla had growing concerns over rescuing the boy alive. No demand for ransom had been made. Based on the outcomes of past cases, Shukla was worried that if the kidnappers were unable to keep seven-year-old Om quiet, they might kill him.

More than nabbing the kidnappers, the police's focus was on rescuing Om safely. Around 200 policemen continuously combed the city to look for the missing child with Shukla closely supervising the developments. With each passing hour, Shukla was unable to shake off the gnawing feeling that the kidnappers may have killed the child. 'I was not able to sleep and was taking an update on the case every two hours. Being a mother myself, how could I? The only question in my mind was whether the boy was still alive since the abductors never allowed the child to speak to his parents,' she said.

After forming separate teams, the police decided to track Sandeep's phone and waited for another call from the kidnapper. Sure enough, the kidnapper called on Sunday morning, 24 September, and made the first demand for a ransom of Rs 60 lakh. He then told the father that he would call again to let him know about the place and time for the drop-off, before abruptly ending the call. The police later found out that of the two, Roshan had made the ransom calls. The analysis of their voice samples and the recordings of the ransom calls, however, are still awaited.

As they waited for the third call, the police urged Sandeep to bargain with the kidnapper to reduce the ransom with the intention of keeping the kidnapper engaged on the call. Following their advice, Sandeep tried to negotiate with the kidnappers by telling them that it was difficult to arrange for such a large sum of money on a Sunday and countered with an offer of Rs 10 lakh.

The kidnappers were adamant and and refused to budge, and they claimed that they knew how wealthy Sandeep was. The negotiations continued over several phone calls, which lasted until 11.30 a.m. on 25 September. 'I tried to explain to them that the money in our business is in the market and we don't have so much money in cash. I told them that I only had Rs 17 lakh. They agreed to settle for Rs 20 lakh. I borrowed the rest from my relatives and arranged for the amount,' said Sandeep.

The police still had a crucial factor to deal with—whether Om was alive or not. This had to be determined as soon as possible. During the negotiation, the police directed Sandeep to ask the kidnapper to let him speak with his son. Surprisingly, the kidnapper obliged. He allowed Om to speak to his father, giving everyone a sign that after almost two days, he was alive and well.

Now that the amount was agreed upon, the kidnappers asked Sandeep to come alone on a scooter instead of in his car. They asked him to reach the Talawade MIDC bridge with the money later that day at 2 p.m.

The voice recordings of the calls gave the police another clue. Senior Inspector Vijay said, 'After listening to him speak in Hindi, we could make out from his accent that he was a Maharashtrian. From our observations, he seemed to be a local resident since he knew the area well, and we started to look for suspects who matched our criteria.' Since Sandeep had a business in electric panels, the police made a list of his business associates who may have had a role to play in his son's kidnapping.

* * *

Following the kidnapper's instructions, the police started their preparations. Inspector Shankar Avtade was to ride pillion with Sandeep. Other policemen would follow them on motorcycles and they would all be dressed in plain clothes.

Around 300 police officials were also working on the case, determined to bring the boy back home alive. The police had arranged themselves in teams at various locations and were stationed at the police commissioner's office on Sadhu Vaswani Road. Check-posts were set up across the city. The increased police presence in the area was visible.

When it was time to meet the kidnappers, Sandeep and Shankar took the scooter and drove to the Talawade MIDC bridge. Even though Shankar was posing as Sandeep's relative, he carried his gun in case things didn't go as planned. Vijay was constantly in touch with Shankar over the phone, and police officers were being positioned near the bridge accordingly.

But the kidnappers had an inkling that the police had got involved. Something was amiss. They had probably noticed the increased police presence as well. They decided to hang back and observe Sandeep from a distance before approaching him.

The kidnappers noticed that there were too many people near the bridge. They got spooked and realized that it was too risky to take the money. They fled from the area with Om.

The police figured that the kidnappers knew the area well and had noticed the unusual traffic movement in the locality. 'Once the kidnappers suspected the police had got involved, they assumed any man on the road was police personnel,' said Vijay.

The kidnappers tried to stay a step ahead of them. The duo went to great lengths to ensure that their car couldn't be easily identified by frequently changing the car's number plate. The police later revealed that Akshay and Roshan had allegedly used three number plates, copied from online advertisements for the sale of used cars. Regardless of the reason, the police had lost their only chance of rescuing the child from the kidnappers.

All hope, however, wasn't lost yet. The police were confident that the kidnappers wouldn't be able to leave the area since there were check-posts set up on all routes leading out of the Talawade MIDC bridge. The noose had been tightened, and the kidnappers realized that there was only one way out of the mess they had created. They weighed their options and decided to abandon their plan. Their priority now was to avoid getting arrested.

Later that evening, they dropped Om off near Sandeep's godown in Newale Vasti. Only after they fled the area did they call Om's father around 8 p.m. to let him know that they had left his son near the godown unharmed. Before hanging up, they told Sandeep that they were no longer interested in the ransom money.

The Kharats cried in relief, but the police still had concerns about the well-being of the boy. Unsure of whether the boy had been left unharmed or dead, Senior Inspector Vijay contacted police officers deputed in that area and asked them to look for the boy near the godown. Within minutes of the phone call, they found Om. A ten-minute car ride later, Om was back in the arms of his mother. For the family, the ordeal had ended. But the police still had a job at hand—to find the suspects who had kidnapped an innocent child to make a quick buck.

After Om reached home, the police asked him to describe the kidnappers and prepared sketches using the details. Om said he recognized one as someone who used to come home. Using the clues they had collected over the past two days, the police were able to piece the rest of the puzzle together.

In cases where the victim is found alive, his or her statement is an important piece of evidence. In this case, after the duo was arrested, the police found that the sketches were an 80 per cent match to the kidnappers' faces.

In the early hours of 26 September, the police arrested Akshay from his house. In the ensuing interrogation, he named Roshan as his accomplice, who was also arrested the same day. The identity of the kidnappers came as a shock to Sandeep. He started to put the pieces together.

Sandeep recalled that Akshay had indeed come home on multiple occasions when he worked as a delivery person around six months ago. 'Up until the time the police revealed his identity, I had not even thought of him as a possible suspect even after speaking to him six or seven times on the phone. He had approached me for a job, and I had hired him to deliver goods to a customer for a monthly salary of Rs 8000,' said Sandeep. Akshay had worked for him for around three months, and he didn't remember having any complaints about him.

Deputy Commissioner of Police Pankaj Dahane said, 'When they were planning the kidnapping, they were confident that the parents wouldn't approach the police and they would get away with it.'[5] As per their plan, Roshan and Akshay allegedly kidnapped Om from outside his home and drove to their village in Gevrai in the Beed district. However, once there, they realized that they needed to recharge their phones in order to make the ransom calls. They didn't want to leave Om at the village unsupervised. So they decided to return to the city, and in order to avoid any police check-posts on the way, took a longer route back.

---

[5] From an interview with Pankaj Dahane in Pune on 7 March 2018.

Police investigation later revealed that in order to reduce the chances of being caught, the kidnappers kept Om in the car since the time they picked him up from his house. They fed him biscuits and other snacks from time to time. They knew that the best way to avoid arousing any suspicion was to treat the child well. The kidnappers simply told him that his father was on his way with the money, after which he could go home. They were careful not to threaten or harm him in any way.

Shukla lauded the boy's courage in staying calm throughout the harrowing experience. A cry of panic or any attempt to draw attention from a passer-by could have easily provoked the kidnappers to forcibly keep him quiet or, worse, kill him.

* * *

The news of their arrests affected Roshan's and Akshay's families more than the Kharat's since they had to suffer the consequences of a crime they had played no part in.

After the incident, both families suffered incessant taunts from their neighbours until they felt they had no other option but to move out of their homes. Roshan's parents moved to another residential area 10 kilometres away from their previous home in Ganesh Nagar in Chikhali. Akshay's parents, who were already struggling to make ends meet, eventually returned to their village in the Beed district.

Roshan's father, Nandkishore Shinde, is still perplexed over what drove his son to commit such a crime. Nandkishore and his family had moved to Pune from his village around ten years ago in the hope of a better life. Nandkishore worked as a senior mechanic with a Maruti service dealership and ran a part-time business selling Ayurvedic products for a company called Lifestyle. It was honest work and earned him enough money to provide a comfortable life for his family.[6]

After schooling, Roshan had tried to set up his career on his own a few times too. He had a brief stint at a Dish TV outlet and then tried his hand at selling Tata Docomo SIM cards. After several such odd jobs, Roshan, an ambitious person, decided to set up his own driving school.

The school began operations a couple of months before the incident. Roshan would give driving lessons and procure a licence for a fee of Rs 2000. He even roped in other people to pool in resources, but the business didn't do very well. Eventually, he shut it down.

Nandkishore grows pensive when he recalls his son's dreams of becoming a rich man without the will to work for it. 'He didn't want to take up a job but had big expectations from life. He wanted to be a rich person with stylish cars and a big house. One has to work very hard for five to ten years before one can achieve them,' said Nandkishore.

Still, Nandkishore was wary about pressuring him to get a job. 'Even though all his friends had taken up jobs, we would never nag him to do so since he was still young and my only child. I always had a fear that if I push him too much, he might do something untoward,' he said. Nandkishore often reasoned with himself that there was no urgency since he earned well, and Roshan could develop his own business when he was ready to start working.

---

[6] From an interview with Nandkishore Shinde in Pune on 12 November 2017.

After Roshan shut down his business, he seemed dejected and kept mostly to himself. On the day Roshan and Akshay set out to kidnap Om, Nandkishore recalls that Roshan had left without informing them. The next they heard about him was after he was arrested by the police. When Roshan didn't return home for two days, his parents didn't think much of it since he had gone on trips with his friends without letting them know on more than a few occasions earlier.

Nandkishore waited for him for three days. Roshan had been upset for days before he left, and his father worried for him. On 26 September, four days after his son left the house, a family friend called around 5 p.m. to tell him about his son's arrest. 'Ever since he shut down his business, I used to call him four times a day just to inquire about what he was doing. I got worried when I wasn't able to reach him for three days. Just when I was thinking of going to the police station, I came to know that he had been arrested. I couldn't believe it. I rushed to the station with my wife to find out what had happened,' he said.

Family members said that Roshan and Akshay had been friends for only a month before they hatched the plan of kidnapping a child for ransom. The police touted Roshan's debts from his driving school as the motive behind the plan.

However, Roshan's father denied the possibility of such a large debt. After Roshan shut his business down, Nandkishore inquired about pending payments and found some customers who had paid fees ranging from Rs 10,000–15,000 and hadn't received their driving licences. He returned the money to the individual customers.

About a fortnight after the business folded, Nandkishore asked his son if there were other losses in the business that needed to be settled. But Roshan denied having any other debts. 'After he was arrested, I asked his partners about any other pending payments as well. They said that there might be pending debts amounting to Rs 50,000. Had Roshan opened up about his problems earlier, all of this could have been avoided,' he said.

Akshay's parents, who were daily-wage labourers, had a tougher ordeal and are still struggling to understand the legal ramifications of their son's actions. Akshay's father, Kashinath Jamdare, relied on daily wages for the sustenance of his wife, Chandrakala, and his three sons, including Akshay. Kashinath took up menial jobs, like driving a Tempo or working as a labourer. In order to support the family income, Akshay's mother worked as a domestic help. The family lived in a *kuchha* house with an asbestos roof near Kudalwadi.

After people came to know about Akshay's alleged involvement in the kidnapping, his parents faced a backlash from their neighbours. 'They are poor and uneducated people. After people came to know about the incident, they would pass comments at his parents and they would get into fights. Considering their poor financial condition, I advised them to move back to their village and they did,' said Krushna Shelke, Akshay's maternal uncle.[7]

Owing to the financial crisis in his sister's family, Krushna took Akshay in with the hope of giving him a chance to build a career for himself. For that, Krushna made sure that he received an education. After completing class X

---

[7]   From an interview with Krushna Shelke in Pune on 11 November 2017.

from Saraswati School, Akshay lived with his uncle's family and went on to finish junior college from Nutan High School.

But things didn't pan out as Krushna had hoped. After junior college, Akshay refused to study further. The disagreement about pursuing further education turned into arguments between Akshay and his uncle. A social worker and a well-known face in the area, Krushna soon found out that Akshay had fallen in with the wrong crowd. He would loiter around the neighbourhood all day with his friends. Unwilling to face criticism from his sister and brother-in-law for having led him astray, Krushna decided that it was in everyone's best interest to send Akshay home.

More than two years before Akshay allegedly kidnapped Om, a frustrated Krushna sent his wayward nephew back to his parents. 'After junior college, I had asked him to join the police academy, following which he would get a job and could support his family. But he refused. He wanted to start a business of his own instead. I didn't approve of his plans and asked him to leave,' he said.

Due to the falling-out between the two, Krushna and his nephew stopped speaking to each other. The next time he heard about his nephew was when the police came knocking at his door looking for Akshay.

While Nandkishore maintains that his son made a terrible mistake, he also thinks that Roshan, who was a final-year B.Com student, was misled by Akshay, who had planned the kidnapping. In his opinion, Roshan didn't realize the implications of his actions until it was too late. 'My son had never done anything of this sort before, and everyone in the neighbourhood knows him as a good and helpful person.

Jamdare was the mastermind behind the plan, and my son was only following his directions,' he insisted.

Much like Nandkishore, Akshay's uncle blames Roshan for leading his nephew astray. Even though the nature of their crime is serious, Krushna hopes that the judge will be lenient towards Akshay and give him another chance, especially since he doesn't have any criminal history.

Vouching for his good character, Krushna said that Akshay grew up in a stable environment and reiterated that he was a helpful person. Even though he did kidnap Om, Krushna argued that Akshay had never intended to harm the boy in any manner. Citing his own example, Krushna pointed out that Akshay took good care of his six-year-old son and eleven-year-old daughter when he was living with them.

While Akshay was growing up, Krushna and his nephew were close. Krushna treated Akshay more like a sibling, making sure that he had everything he needed without having to ask for it. Apart from clothes and shoes, Krushna recalls buying him a two-wheeler and mobile phones as well.

Incidentally, a message about the missing child was doing the rounds on WhatsApp groups and Krushna had helped spread the word. 'I had no idea that a member of my family was behind it, and I was stunned when I came to know about it. I feel really helpless now watching him pleading for help,' he said.

In the meetings he had with his son at Yerwada Jail, Roshan told his father that he thoroughly repents his actions. 'He would tell me that he made a mistake because of Akshay and that given a chance, he would never do such a thing again. What happened cannot be changed, and he will have to suffer the consequences of it. But many people who go to jail are not hardened criminals and neither is our son. It was in his destiny, so he had to go to jail,' Nandkishore said. As a father, he hopes that his son will get a shorter term of imprisonment since the child was returned alive and unharmed.

After being interrogated for several hours, the police said that the duo spilled the beans on their nearly flawless plan. The police claimed that while Roshan wanted to settle the debt he had incurred due to his failing business, Akshay wanted to fulfil his dreams of being a rich man.

Apart from stealing the SIM card from Chavan's phone, the two also allegedly admitted that they chose Om particularly because they were aware of the details of Sandeep's business and income. It came to light that while they had both planned to kidnap a child, it was Akshay's idea to kidnap Om.

The Nigdi police filed a charge sheet against the two accused on 19 December 2017. Unlike in other cases where one of the accused persons is considered the main culprit, in this case, the police believe that both had an equal role to play in the crime. The offence committed by them, kidnapping for ransom, amounts to an imprisonment term ranging between a minimum of three years and a maximum of ten.

Despite the serious nature of their crime, the police officials noted that the kidnappers treated the child well and did not intend to kill him. Based on the statement given by Om, they didn't tie his hands. They simply made him sit in the car and fed him from time to time.

The statement indicates that they even took him to Monginis and bought him pastries. 'The boy didn't quite understand the gravity of the situation he was in, and probably that is why he was perfectly calm when we found him near his father's godown,' said Vijay.

Like the SIM card they used to make the ransom calls and the duplicate number plates, the duo used a car that did not belong to them. Based on their confession, the police said that Roshan was planning to purchase a car hoping to revive his driving school business. For that, he had struck a deal with the owner of the Indica Vista.

He kept the car with the promise of paying for it soon. 'He had been using the car for nearly a month while the payment was still pending. After we arrested them, they confessed that they had hidden the car and parked it in an open ground in Purnanagar. We recovered the car and recorded the statement of the owner,' said an official from the Nigdi police station.

* * *

Pune Police Commissioner Shukla insists that since a majority of kidnapping cases involve someone known to the family, parents should keep a close eye on friends, employees and other frequent visitors.

Even though the Kharats and the police could not have hoped for a better ending, the experience has left an indelible mark on Om. Understandably shaken from his ordeal, he is reluctant to step out of the house. 'We were in a state of constant fear, and after he came back home, we did not send him to school for around ten days. Later, we realized that keeping him at home may not be good for his mental health and decided that following the regular routine would be better,' said Sandeep.

The boy who loved playing with his friends now prefers to stay indoors. 'While we try not to broach the topic too much, we can see that he is scared that someone else might come and take him away. Even if he steps out, he plays for about ten minutes and then wants to go back inside,' he said.

Sandeep hopes that given Om's young age, time will cure his fear. He is even considering taking him to a counsellor. As parents, the three days were nightmarish for Sandeep and his wife, but the experience has taught him a few lessons. He has now decided to be alert and is careful of the people he interacts with.

Nigdi's sleepy neighbourhood has gone back to being its normal self, but for the Kharats, the streets will never be the same again.

* * *

Om's story came as a relief while I was looking for cases that ended differently—where the children who were kidnapped managed to return home unharmed. It somehow restored a certain sense of faith in the efforts taken up by the police to compel the kidnappers to release the boy alive.

Despite the best outcome, Om's father is understandably more protective of his family and takes extra precautions to ensure that the safety of his family is not compromised. During our meeting, Sandeep had asked my opinion on a particular matter, as would any father in his shoes. He told me that ever since the incident, he has been toying with the idea of shifting to another place to eliminate all chances of another similar occurrence and asked me if I thought it would help.

Thinking of what many senior police officials had told me during previous interviews, I told him that there was virtually no way for him to foresee or prevent his son from getting kidnapped. One cannot be aware of possible grudges that an acquaintance may hold on to, let alone pre-empt their actions. Any precautions that Sandeep could take at another house could be taken at his current residence as well.

Unlike most cases where a child doesn't make it back home, in Om's case, the police had something they are rarely able to add to their evidence list—Om's statement as a witness. Eventually, the court will decide whether Roshan and Akshay were indeed guilty of the allegations levelled against them. Regardless of the judgment, I hope Om returns to his playful self and this distressing experience does not pose a hindrance in his life.

10

Anant Gupta, Noida

On 19 November 2006, twenty-year-old Chhatrapal Singh, who had dreamt of being an actor, found himself in a police lock-up, being interrogated by Sub-Inspector Sushil Kumar Dubey over the kidnapping of a three-year-old boy from Noida on 13 November.[1]

'*Kyun, be, teri haiseeyat hai kya pachaas lakh rupaye maangne ki* (So, you think you have the status to demand Rs 50 lakh)?' Dubey thundered at the cowering man.

'*Nahi, saab, maine toh sirf paanch lakh mangi thi. Unhone pachaas lakh suna* (No, sir, I had asked for only Rs 5 lakh. She heard it as Rs 50 lakh),' replied Chhatrapal.

If it was comedy acting he aspired to, he certainly had the timing for it.

The missing three-year-old boy, Anant, was the son of Naresh Gupta, then managing director of Adobe India. Around 9 a.m. on 13 November, a Monday, Anant stepped

---

[1] Interview with Sushil Kumar Dubey in New Delhi on 6 February 2018.

211

out of his home in a gated society in Noida's Sector 15A
to catch his school bus at 8.50 a.m. The bus stop was just
50 metres away and with Anant was Seema Devi, the Guptas'
domestic help. A pre-nursery student at Lotus Valley School,
Anant was eager to meet his friends.

Barely forty steps from the gate, Seema noticed two men
on a black Hero Honda Splendour. They stopped in front of
Seema and Anant, blocking their path. In a split second, the
man riding pillion grabbed Anant and the bike sped away.
Instinctively, Seema screamed for help and her cries were
heard by the guard, Kameshwar Ojha, and passers-by. Ojha
and other people tried in vain to chase down the bike, which
made a quick U-turn and disappeared through one of the
society's main gates.

Unfortunately, neither of Anant's parents were home at
the time. His mother, Nidhi, had left the house at 8.30 a.m.
for Marwah Studios in Sector 16A, where she was pursuing a
master's course in mass communication, while her husband,
Naresh, was on his way back from a business trip to San
Francisco.

Without wasting any time, Kameshwar quickly telephoned
the police and told them what had happened. Within a few
minutes a police team arrived at the house, and by 9.40 a.m., a
kidnapping complaint had been registered at Sector 20 Noida
police station.

Nidhi heard the news from a neighbour about half an
hour later while she was in her class and rushed back home.
By then, the police had begun questioning eyewitnesses, and
Nidhi and her relatives could do little but wait anxiously.

Naresh was in Hong Kong, waiting to board a flight to
Delhi, when his brother-in-law, Lalit Kumar Gupta, called

to tell him what had happened. After the initial reaction of shock, he knew he had no time to waste. He began calling his friends at once, who rushed to the airport in Hong Kong.

It wasn't long before word spread to senior police officers, politicians and even the Prime Minister's Office. Everyone involved knew that the stakes were high. Meanwhile, with Anant sandwiched between them, the kidnappers, Chhatrapal and his accomplice, Pavan Pal, rode 400 kilometres to Hardoi. On the way, they gave Anant guavas, warning him that they wouldn't take him back home if he cried or didn't eat them.

They stopped at the home of Pavan Pal's relative, Ram Dayal, and spent the night there. The next day, 14 November, they set out for Etah, a town located 180 kilometres away, where they planned to spend the day at the home of Chhatrapal's friend, Sunil Yadav. They had decided not to spend too much time in one place, and the next day, 15 November, they paid a visit to Chhatrapal's aunt, Santosh Singh, in Nagla Kashi, Mathura. They spent two days here.

Back in Noida, the Guptas were anxiously awaiting news about their son. It was 6 p.m. when they got a call on their landline. Nidhi answered the call nervously. The man on the other end of the line was abrupt. 'We have your son. Once we get the money, he will be returned to you,' he said before disconnecting the call.

Nidhi waited near the phone hoping for further instructions from the kidnappers. The second call came at 8.45 p.m., and this time, Nidhi asked the man to let her speak to her son. He refused, claiming the boy was unwell.

He once again demanded a ransom but this time was more specific. Nidhi would have to pay Rs 5 lakh in bundles of 500-rupee notes if she wanted to see her son alive again.

Nidhi, however, misheard the sum. She told the police that the kidnapper had demanded a Rs 50 lakh ransom for Anant. Over the next couple of days, the kidnapper telephoned the Guptas a few more times to discuss specifics of the ransom payment.

The police, meanwhile, began following the most obvious lead that they had, the mobile number from which the ransom calls were made. They quickly learnt that the kidnappers were from Noida. A scan of the call records from that number suggested that the kidnapping wasn't the work of organized criminals or the result of a corporate rivalry, but rather the work of amateurs. This was both good and bad news. While amateurs would be easier to deal with, Rajesh said, their inexperience made it more likely that they would panic and kill the child.

The investigation also revealed that the SIM card had been issued to a man named Pravin Kapoor on 5 October 2006. The police soon had his ID proof and address, and paid him a visit. Pravin, they learnt, was a driver who visited Sector 15A frequently and had befriended a man named Jitendra Singh. He told the police that in a bid to help his friend, he had given Jitendra a copy of his driver's licence to use as identity proof for a SIM card. The police had their first suspect.

Their next step was to track the movements of the kidnappers, who were still making phone calls from the same number. The police were able to track the IMEI number.

By the time Naresh reached New Delhi, around 2 a.m. on 14 November, the police hadn't made much headway. Sushil, the sub-inspector with the special operations group of the crime branch, travelled to the airport to meet him on his arrival in Mumbai. Because of the family's wealth and the high-profile nature of Naresh's job, the kidnapping had already been widely reported in the media, and the family had to deal with incessant queries. Naresh, as reported in an article published by *Business Standard*, implored the media not to reveal the latest developments in the case as this could further jeopardize his son's life.[2]

He also made it perfectly clear to the police that money was no object and that he wanted his son back alive at any cost. 'They told us that we could negotiate down the ransom amount but we didn't want to. We were prepared to give any sum of money,' said Naresh.

Naresh even hired a US-based expert who specialized in negotiating with kidnappers. He flew in from the Philippines after he heard about the incident to help the Guptas and the police deal with the situation more efficiently. He tried to prepare Naresh, guiding him on how best to respond to the kidnappers' demands. His advice was simple—chillingly so—but practically impossible to follow. To get the upper hand, Naresh would have to take emotion out of the equation and treat the exchange like a business transaction.

Naresh recounted, 'He had a lot of experience with such cases and told me that once contact had been made with the kidnapper, it was a simple transaction. I had something they wanted and they had something I wanted. I remember him telling me that since I was a businessman, I would understand this.'[3]

---

[2] http://www.business-standard.com/article/economy-policy/little-headway-in-kidnapping-case-106111501132_1.html

[3] From an interview with Naresh Gupta in New Delhi on 31 January 2018.

The consultant also insisted that Naresh get proof from the kidnappers that his son was still alive, as many kidnapping cases in India turn into murders. After much back and forth, the kidnappers acceded. Naresh was allowed to speak to Anant at 10.50 a.m. In the brief conversation, Naresh said his son was well and sounded almost cheerful—possibly because he was too young to understand what had happened. He told his father he had been in the fields with dogs, ducks and buffaloes.

Behind the scenes, a team from the Special Task Force was tasked with finding and chasing down leads in parallel with the local police. The police were also given specialist surveillance equipment to help track the kidnappers through their mobile phone. Though in common use today, this technology was rarely deployed in 2006. From their mobile phone location, the police learnt that the kidnappers were travelling from Aligarh to Mathura. A police team was dispatched to the highway but could not track them down. The police had no luck finding them since they expected the kidnappers to take a car while travelling for such a long distance. But the kidnappers had continued on the same motorcycle with Anant seated between them. The police claimed that by 15 November, they had figured out who the kidnappers were but had to keep their distance until the child was rescued to avoid provoking them.

Once the police had proof that Anant was still alive, communication with the kidnappers moved on to the manner of handing over the ransom. This, however, proved far from straightforward. Over several phone calls, the kidnappers ordered Naresh to bring the money to different places, changing their mind each time. Naresh guessed that it was a ploy to confuse them and show them who was in control. 'He told us to bring the money to Bhopal, then to Delhi, Ahmedabad, Mumbai and Jaipur. The police told us that we wouldn't know the final location until the last minute,' said Naresh. Not one to be caught unprepared, Naresh instructed bankers in all five cities to keep a bag with Rs 50 lakh in cash ready.

Around 2 p.m. on 16 November, the kidnappers telephoned Naresh and told him to bring the money to Delhi's Hazrat Nizamuddin railway station in fifteen minutes. But there was a catch. The kidnappers wanted Naresh himself to bring the money. Naresh tried to explain that there was no way he could do so without alerting the throng of journalists outside their home who would surely follow him. The kidnappers, however, were not willing to listen and disconnected the call.

But they called back and eventually relented. 'They finally agreed to allow Lalit, my brother-in-law, to bring the money instead,' said Naresh. The kidnapper called again at 4.15 p.m. to check whether Lalit was on his way. Accompanied by a security guard, Lalit left for Nizamuddin railway station with Nidhi's mobile phone and Rs 50 lakh in a black bag. He said that the kidnappers had told him to board the Dehradun Express, which was headed to Mumbai, and await further instructions.

A few hours later, Lalit and the guard boarded the train and were soon on their way. The next time the kidnapper called, around 3 a.m. on 17 November, they were close to Mathura railway station. Sushil recounted the scene, which could well be straight out of a movie, 'The kidnapper told Lalit to stand at the door of the train. He said they would wait

at the drain and shine a torch from below to show him where
to toss the bag.'

The Guptas' lawyer, B.R. Sharma, said they knew things
could go very wrong if others on the train knew the two were
carrying Rs 50 lakh in cash.[4] He said Naresh was willing to
pay ten times the ransom demanded and rejected the police's
suggestion to use fake notes as he didn't want to risk his son's
life. He added that as a precautionary measure, while Lalit was
on the train, a car was sent to follow it with a bag containing
an additional Rs 50 lakh in case the kidnappers increased the
ransom or something went wrong on the train. Meanwhile,
Naresh, who was monitoring the situation with his brother-
in-law, became increasingly tense. What if the kidnappers
didn't get the money? What would they do to his son?

Around 8 a.m. on 17 November, after what seemed like
forever, the kidnappers telephoned Lalit. They said they had
received the money and that Anant was somewhere on the
train that Lalit had boarded. Lalit called Naresh at once to
inform him and looked in every compartment of the train.
But after a thorough search, he told Naresh that Anant was
not on the train: the kidnapper had lied. Naresh and his wife
frantically tried to call the kidnapper back. Eventually, they
answered the call and told Naresh to go to Mumbai, where he
would meet his son.

All we know for sure from this point in time is that Anant
was not in Mumbai either. Around three hours after Naresh
last spoke to the kidnappers, his son was returned home,
unharmed. Amid the relief over Anant's return, the story of

---

[4] From an interview with B.R. Sharma in New Delhi on 1 February
2018.

how this came about, however, is murky at best and sparked a controversy in the media back in 2006.

In one version of events, as Naresh was packing for Mumbai, an autorickshaw pulled up outside his home and out stepped Anant. The kidnappers, it turned out, had taken him to Mathura—he was with them when they picked up the money. Keeping up their end of the bargain, they then brought him back to Noida, put him in an autorickshaw, paid the driver Rs 500 and told him where to take the child. This version of events, espoused by Chhatrapal's advocate, Hari Raj Singh, in court, was backed up off the record by a police official who was on the investigating team. The official said, 'When [the kidnappers] reached Apollo Hospital in Noida, they put Anant in an autorickshaw, gave the driver Anant's address and Rs 500 and told him to drop the boy back home.'

The official version of events that made it to the charge sheet, however, was considerably different.[5] According to the police, a team led by Brajesh Pratap Singh, the officer in charge of the case, rescued Anant from a jungle in Salempur, Uttar Pradesh, after receiving a tip-off. According to Brajesh's statement, around 10 a.m. on 17 November, half a kilometre into the jungle, they saw a boy crying on the side of the road. Brajesh said he got out of the vehicle, approached the child and soon realized it was Anant. He said the boy had an identity card hanging around his neck with his name and the name of his school—Lotus Valley. He said out of fear of being caught,

[5] Based on the court order *The State vs Chhatrapal Singh, Jitendra Singh & Pavan Pal*, Sessions Case No. 127 of 2007 (District Court [SC/ST Act], Gautam Buddh Nagar, 26 September 2011).

the kidnappers had apparently left him there and fled. The police maintained that it was Brajesh who returned Anant to his parents around noon that day.

With Anant back home safely, the police concentrated their efforts on finding the kidnappers. Around 4 a.m. that day, they arrested Jitendra near a Bharat Petroleum pump near Noida Circle. Upon interrogation, Jitendra told the police that he and his brother, Chhatrapal, had come up with the idea of kidnapping Anant for money and had convinced their friend Pavan Pal, a daily-wage labourer, to be a part of their plan. From him, the police learnt that the two men on the bike who had snatched Anant were Chhatrapal and Pavan. Jitendra's role in the kidnapping was that of a lookout—he was stationed in front of the Guptas' home to give his brother updates about the police.

He also told the police that earlier that day, Chhatrapal had hidden the bag with the ransom money in their home at Bailana. He led the police to a room on the upper floor of his house, where they found bundles of 500-rupee notes totalling Rs 47.3 lakh in a red bag hidden inside a tin box. Where was the missing Rs 2.7 lakh?

Two days after they arrested his brother, the police picked up Chhatrapal from his house in New Ashok Nagar around 4 p.m. Sub-Inspector Sushil, who remembers the day clearly, said, 'We found him drunk and passed out on the floor. There were two small empty bottles of alcohol lying nearby. We found around Rs 20,000 in 500-rupee notes in his pockets.' The police also found two phones—a Nokia and a Motorola—in his pockets. These were later confirmed to be the phones the kidnappers had used to make the ransom calls, but Rs 2.5 lakh was still unaccounted for.

The police said Chhatrapal in turn led them to Pavan, whom they tracked down using his mobile tower location. They arrested him from his home in Hardoi on 26 November.[6]

Chhatrapal also told the police that he had discarded the black bag containing the Rs 50 lakh ransom near Mathura. He showed them the area, and the empty bag was found in some bushes near the railway track on 24 November.

A police official, who did not wish to be named, said a colleague who had helped recover the bag told him that it had a large tear, implying that some of the money may have slipped out. Chhatrapal's advocate, Hari, however, said he was confident the police had pocketed the money.[7]

Apart from Chhatrapal, Jitendra and Pavan, the police arrested four of their relatives, suspecting they may have been accomplices in the crime by giving sanctuary to the kidnappers. Those arrested were twenty-eight-year-old Vir Singh, his wife, Santosh, also twenty-eight, from Nangla Kashi in Mathura; twenty-eight-year-old Sunil Kumar from Etah; and sixty-year-old Ram Dayal from Hardoi.

Though he hadn't spoken to either of the kidnappers on the phone, Naresh said later that he felt sympathy for Pavan and his family despite the gravity of the crime and believed he had been led astray by Chhatrapal. 'We later found out that Pavan had treated Anant very well and that he had urged Chhatrapal to return Anant to us even if they didn't get the money,' he said. Pavan hailed from a poor family and had earlier worked as a daily-wage labourer.

---

[6] https://www.telegraphindia.com/1061127/asp/nation/story_7055553.asp

[7] From an interview with Hari Raj Singh in New Delhi on 10 February 2018.

In his statement to the police, Chhatrapal said they had stolen the motorbike that they used to kidnap Anant from Delhi. Based on the information he gave, they found the bike in a parking lot at Ghaziabad railway station. Near it, the police said, they found a white plastic bag that contained a card with a photo of Anant and his address on one side and a photo and address of Seema, the family's domestic help, on the other.

The police investigation found that Chhatrapal, the mastermind, was inspired by various movies. The police described Chhatrapal as an 'overambitious person' who had acted in a telefilm and wanted to try his hand at movies.[8]

Years after the kidnapping, however, one question continues to trouble Naresh. Why did the kidnappers choose Anant? Yes, he was from a rich family, but the Guptas have never showed off their wealth and certainly weren't the only well-to-do family in the neighbourhood.

The kidnappers themselves never explained why they chose Anant and maintained that he was a random target. Naresh said, 'They told the police that they had no particular target and were just roaming around when they saw Anant. We know that is not true because we learnt they had done a recce of the area a week before the kidnapping.' He also pointed to Seema's statement to the police, in which she said that a week before Anant was kidnapped, the same two men had brushed past them on their bike. At the time, she thought they were harassing her and only later realized that they must have been the same men who kidnapped Anant.

---

[8] https://www.outlookindia.com/newswire/story/main-accused-and-accomplice-in-anant-kidnapping-case-arrested/430703

After much thought, however, Naresh recalled an incident that happened a few months before Anant was kidnapped that might explain why the kidnappers chose his son.

He said he had bought a mobile phone for his wife, Nidhi, which she left behind in the car. It got stolen, and Naresh suspected that the man who washed their car had taken it as he had access to the car. However, he denied having stolen the phone when Naresh confronted him the next day. 'Now there is a part of me that says I should have called the cops and handed him over. I could have done that based on the hunch I had but decided to let it go. My guard told this story to some other people, and maybe word spread that we were soft targets,' he said.

* * *

According to the police, Chhatrapal, Jitendra and Pavan together worked out the plan to kidnap Anant. For this, Chhatrapal and Jitendra sought information from their father, Satpal Singh, about the Guptas' daily routine. Satpal, a retired army officer, owned a Mother Dairy booth near the Guptas' home, and Anant's school bus stopped right in front of it. Satpal, however, had no idea about his sons' intentions.

The police said Chhatrapal, the leader, thought that it would be a good idea for one of them to keep an eye on the developments at the Guptas' home after the other two had kidnapped Anant. His brother, Jitendra, was assigned this role since he often worked at his father's Mother Dairy booth and could linger around the house without arousing suspicion.

The prosecution called in nineteen witnesses, including Kameshwar and Seema. Advocate B.R. Sharma said that as

Anant was only three years old at the time of the incident, there was some concern whether his testimony would be admissible in court. But, he added, the judge personally assessed whether Anant could remember the details of the incident before allowing his testimony to be used as evidence, the most important one of the lot. The suspects' voice samples were also analysed and compared to the recordings of the ransom calls.

In his statement, Anant said that though he didn't know the date on which he was kidnapped, he did remember that he was on his way to school with Seema when two men on a motorcycle grabbed him. He identified Chhatrapal and Pavan in court but not Jitendra. Among the others who were arrested, the only other suspect he recognized was Chhatrapal's aunt, Santosh. He said he had spent two days at her house and that she had fed him and treated him well.

The boy's vivid memory of his four-day ordeal helped the police build their case. Naresh said, 'Anant remembered that the aunt [Santosh] had sat him on her lap and fed him rotis. She even gave him Rs 50 as a token of her blessing. He remembered playing with their goats as well. They had to treat him well. Had he cried the whole time, he would have attracted unwanted attention.' He also said that at each of the places where they hid Anant, his captors introduced him as a friend's nephew to avoid raising suspicion. Despite everything, Naresh acknowledged the fact that the kidnappers had treated his son well under the given circumstances and that this meant Anant did not suffer long-term trauma.

As serious as their crimes were, none of the three were hardened criminals. While Chhatrapal had a few petty crime cases, including thefts, registered against him, Jitendra and Pavan had a clean record. It was obvious that Chhatrapal had made promises of earning a quick buck to convince them to be a part of his plan.

A series of mistakes by the amateur kidnappers eventually led to them getting caught. For one, they used the same Nokia handset for the personal SIM card and to make the ransom calls, which allowed the police to determine Jitendra's identity and track their movements with relative ease.

But this wasn't the biggest mistake they made. Naresh recalled that the kidnappers once telephoned his landline from a personal number, and asked him to purchase some talktime for it. This, more than anything, convinced the police that they weren't dealing with professional kidnappers.

Rajesh Pandey, one of the six members of the Special Task Force team, said that based on his experience of kidnapping cases, abducting very young children was always fraught with risk. 'In an hour or two, the child will start crying for his or her mother and raise the suspicions of a neighbour or passer-by, who might ask whose child it is.'[9]

He may have lacked the expertise of a career criminal, but Chhatrapal was not one to give up. On 4 February 2008, when he was brought to the court in Noida, he managed to escape even as his shocked mother and sister-in-law looked on. 'He escaped after the hearing, perhaps knowing that he was sure to be convicted. He had bribed a policeman who was in charge of bringing him to the court to not handcuff him while he was there. He saw a chance and made a dash for it,' said B.R. Sharma.

---

[9] From a telephonic conversation with Rajesh Pandey on 7 February 2018.

The police searched for Chhatrapal for two months before eventually finding him on 3 April 2008.[10] After escaping, he kept dodging the police. B.R. Sharma said that Chhatrapal had, in the meantime, got his hands on some saffron robes, grown a beard and was hiding in plain sight as a sadhu at a temple. A newspaper report mentioned that Chhatrapal was arrested from his home in Rabupura,[11] his native town, by a special operations group of Uttar Pradesh police.

Hari, the lawyer representing Chhatrapal, maintained that all three men had been falsely implicated in the case. He alleged that the police had doctored Anant's statement and shown him pictures of Chhatrapal, Pavan and Jitendra while teaching him to say their names in court.

He claimed the police had altered the facts. He rejected their claim, included in the charge sheet, that they found Anant in a forest, saying the boy had returned home in an autorickshaw. He added, 'Because of the pressure created by the media and the high-profile nature of the case, the judiciary becomes biased, which is reflected in this judgment. In such cases, people are falsely implicated and the real culprits get away.'

The other discrepancies he pointed out involved the statement of Jitendra and Chhatrapal's father, Satpal, who mentioned that both of them had started working at the Mother Dairy booth earlier that year. Satpal also said that the police had come asking about Anant on 15 November. 'Satpal

---

[10] http://www.thehindu.com/todays-paper/tp-national/three-get-life-term-for-2006-kidnapping-of-adobe-ceos-son/article2488989.ece

[11] https://mumbaimirror.indiatimes.com/news/india/abductor-of-ex-adobe-ceos-son-held/articleshow/15799308.cms

had clearly said that the police had picked up Chhatrapal and Jitendra on 16 November and accused them of kidnapping Anant. How could that be true when the police claim that they rescued Anant from them the next day?' said Hari.

Five years had passed by the time the trial at the sessions court in Gautam Buddh Nagar ended. The judgment came on 24 September 2011 in which Sunil, Ram, Santosh and Vir were acquitted. While the judge, Navin Srivastava, held Chhatrapal, Pavan and Jitendra as guilty and sentenced them to life imprisonment, he stated that there wasn't enough evidence to prove the charges of wrongfully keeping a kidnapped person in confinement against the remaining four accused.

In November 2011, shortly after the judgment was pronounced in the sessions court, all three convicts appealed against their life sentences in a petition to the Allahabad High Court. They are now in Luksar prison in Kasna.

Kameshwar Singh, the prosecution lawyer, said that the defence produced no new evidence in court but claimed that the case against the three men was bogus and based on fake evidence. 'They claimed that the prosecution failed to prove guilt beyond reasonable doubt and that the court's findings were not sustainable in the eyes of the law. They said the three men had no connection with the kidnapping and had been falsely implicated,' he said.[12] The high court case was in its final stages and a judgment is expected soon.

* * *

[12] From a telephonic interview with Kameshwar Singh on 30 May 2018.

Twelve years have now passed since he was kidnapped, and Anant is a class X student at Lotus Valley School. Though he has suffered no major long-term trauma, Naresh says Anant is still afraid of the dark. The youngest of three children, he is very social and loves sports, especially tennis and basketball, and computer games.

Naresh and his wife, Nidhi, now try to help families who have gone through the same experience by counselling them. Looking back on that day when he came close to losing his son, Naresh remembers that there were other factors that worked to the kidnappers' advantage. He feels that the kidnappers were able to pull off their plan only because it was a Monday, the day of the week when the Sports and Culture Club located opposite their house was closed. He pointed out that the club had seven security guards and the area was crowded on other days, making it impossible for anyone to grab a child from the street on a motorbike and speed away without getting caught.

One thing he learnt from the ordeal is that while the police can take measures to reduce things like organized crime and the trafficking of children, there is little they can do to prevent random kidnappings such as Anant's, and the onus to protect children rests squarely on their parents. 'The key message is this: protect your personal information and don't come across as soft. Security guards and drivers can spread information that may not appear harmful but could turn out to be, as it did in our case,' he said.

Naresh added that after the incident, he studied several kidnapping cases and found that in many of them, the kidnapper was someone who lived or worked within 50 metres of the victim's house and in some cases had access to it.

He added, 'Kidnapping seems like an easy crime but it is very hard to take to completion. Of course, there is always the risk that the kidnapper will kill the hostage, but successful kidnappings for ransom are rare.' Given the technology available to the police these days, kidnappings are almost impossible to get away with, he added. The simple act of communicating with the victim's family allows the police to track the kidnappers' location and usually leads to their downfall.

Naresh feels that there is a need for the mandatory use of technology by the police, which needs to be updated constantly across the country.

* * *

Anant's case grabbed headlines in every newspaper and television news channel for several months after he was reunited with his family. Most people who have grown up in New Delhi are likely to have a faint recollection of the incident. Therefore, I wanted to ensure that this case is included in the book.

Being the oldest among the ten case studies, it took me several months to track down the details and contact numbers of Anant's family and the police officials who were involved in the case. Similar to Yash Lakhotia's case, while Anant's father, Naresh Gupta, helped me with the details regarding the chronology of events, I had to rely heavily on the court order to document the legal proceedings of the case that eventually led to the conviction of the three accused persons.

Apart from being a high-profile case, Anant's case also had several gaps in the narrative that left many questions unanswered, which added an interesting edge to the case. While the police officials who were a part of the investigation were understandably fuzzy on the precise details of an incident that occurred twelve years ago, the mystery around the manner in which Anant returned home that baffled journalists even back then still remains unsolved. Taking these anomalies into account, the defence counsel raised some good points, which made the trial a compelling one for me to focus on.

By the time I finished writing the book, it became clear to me that there isn't really a way to prevent or reduce such kidnapping cases. But it didn't stop me from hoping that like Om and Anant, more of the victims would come back home safe in the end.

Acknowledgements

Since the day S. Hussain Zaidi, my former reporting head at *Mumbai Mirror*, called me to ask if I ever thought of writing a book, I have had my apprehensions about whether I would do a decent job of it. Documenting cases of children being kidnapped seemed like a grim subject at first but it was something many hadn't written about. A closer look at some of the cases convinced me that their stories definitely needed to be told.

The first step was to identify the case studies, and I drew up a list of ten well-known cases from eight cities that were extensively reported in the media. Before anything else, I had to get in touch with the police, the families of the victims, the lawyers, the accused and any other relevant witnesses who could add colour to the narrative. What I thought would be the easiest part of the whole project, however, turned out to be a rather frustrating affair. Even with the help of friends and colleagues, it took me several months to track down the people I had to interview.

Despite being a journalist for the past eight years, I had never covered crime exclusively and the chance to learn something new seemed like a compelling offer. To top it all, there was the added challenge of travelling alone in cities I had never visited before or knew little about. But fortunately, the stars aligned every time I hit a roadblock and the whole process taught me many valuable lessons for life.

My rather long list of people whom I can't thank enough for helping me through this journey begins with S. Hussain Zaidi, who gave me this incredible opportunity to try my hand at something new. He somehow believed that I would be able to pull this off and would give him ten complete chapters at the end of it. Striking a careful balance, Mr Zaidi guided me whenever I reached out for help, while also giving me the freedom to write the chapters the way I envisioned it.

I would also like to thank Milee Ashwarya, the editor-in-chief at Penguin Random House India, for giving me a chance to explore this subject and taking the time to guide me in the right direction.

While writing multiple stories in a day has never been a challenge for me, working on a lengthy chapter was a whole different ball game altogether. Even with my detailed notes, translating my thoughts into words in an appropriate manner was quite a struggle in the initial stages. What followed were rounds of editing and re-editing the sentences several times over. At the end of ten chapters, I finally understood that in comparison to newspaper articles, writing a book required a different perspective of the narrative.

For that, I have Zaheer Merchant to thank. Apart from patiently answering all my queries and editing the chapters, he stood by me on days I felt thoroughly uninspired as he did on days of triumph when I would finish a chapter. Without him I would have taken a lot longer to complete what seemed to be a mammoth task at first.

I am indebted to my friends who contributed in their own way to keep me motivated. Yolande D'mello, always the friend in need, helped me visualize the larger picture and is the best sounding board I could have hoped for.

The unfailing support of my friends Radhika Ramaswamy, Tanushree Venkatraman and Jendi Kepple, who were ever ready with their words of encouragement whenever my enthusiasm faltered.

Sadaf Modak, Mohammed Thaver, Srinath Rao, my former colleagues at the *Indian Express*, as well as Jitendra Sharma from Zee Media, were indispensable resources every step of the way. Despite their busy schedules, they were always just a call away as I often relied on their expertise in crime reporting and matters pertaining to the courts.

Yogesh Sadhwani, a friend and journalist I always look up to, patiently reasoned things out with me on occasions when I was in a dilemma and gave me the sound advice I knew I could always count on.

Though in the past, many of my colleagues had written a book while working full time in newspapers, it didn't quite work out for me in the same way. When I started working on the book, I was a city reporter with the *Indian Express* and was writing about the civic corporation of Mumbai.

I knew that I needed time to travel and before long I realized that it would come down to a choice. I could either focus on my job or on the book. As difficult as the decision was, I opted to take some time off from city reporting to complete the book. I would like to thank my superiors at the *Indian Express* and *Mid-Day* for being so supportive and encouraging.

I am thankful to Diia Rajan, Jyotsna Singh and other friends and family members for opening up their homes to me during the months I spent travelling.

My aim has been to document the cases as accurately and in as much detail as possible. All the people mentioned in the chapters are real and only the names of the victims of rape, juvenile offenders and their relatives have been changed to protect their identity as mandated by the law.

I am thankful to all the officers of the police force who took the time to explain the various aspects of their investigation in great detail. I am thoroughly grateful to the family members of the victims who were brave enough to recount their painful experiences for me. I realize that none of it could have been easy. I hope that the book does justice to the memories of the victims and of those who could not be rescued in time.